People and Shopping

A Social Background

MOLLY HARRISON

LONDON / ERNEST BENN LIMITED
TOTOWA/NEW JERSEY/ROWMAN AND LITTLEFIELD

First published 1975 by Ernest Benn Limited
25 New Street Square, Fleet Street, London EC4A 3JA
& Sovereign Way, Tonbridge, Kent TN9 1RW

Distributed in Canada by
The General Publishing Company Limited, Toronto

© Molly Harrison 1975
Book designed by Kenneth Day

Printed in Great Britain
ISBN 0 510-12523-9 (U.K.)

Title page shows an American shop sign advertising baked
beans, painted 1886

First published in the United States 1975
by Rowman and Littlefield, Totowa, N.J.

Library of Congress Cataloging in Publication Data

Harrison, Molly.
   People and shopping.
   Bibliography: p. 139
   Includes index.

      1. Shopping—History.   2. Retail trade—History.
   1. Title.

HF5429. H294   1975   381   74-28057
ISBN 0-87471-629-2 (U.S.A.)

For J.B., wise friend and
enthusiastic companion, with
affection and gratitude.

Who buys hath need of a hundred eyes,
who sells hath enough of one
Italian proverb

Contents

1 *Perspective and Evidence*

WORDSWORTH COMPLAINED THAT 'getting and spending we lay waste our powers'. In his sonnet the poet was juxtaposing a love of nature with a love of material *things*, and most of us have probably agreed, at some time or another, that the world is, indeed, 'too much with us' and that we have acquired too many possessions. When we are worried or unhappy nature is certainly a balm, and at times we may feel, too, that the medieval ideal of poverty as a positive virtue to be sought after has a good deal to recommend it.

Yet this ideal is far, immeasurably far, from the practice in Western, urban, industrial societies. There are few people who do not enjoy good things – acquiring them, owning them, giving them, replacing them. And this seems to have been so ever since men and women learned to produce more than they and their families needed, and discovered the advantages and satisfaction of barter. A primitive market, an oasis for caravans of merchants' camels, a Moroccan souk – these are all far removed from what we, today, call 'shopping' but their purpose was, and still is, the same: 'getting and spending'.

Wherever we live, whoever we are, our shopping is very much a reflection of ourselves. What we buy, how we arrange our belongings, whether we keep them for a long time or renew them often – all this is a part of us and a reflection of the society in which we live. Everybody likes to have enough, but 'enough' is a very relative term, its meaning differing entirely from place to place and from one period, one century, to another. The desperately little possessed by the majority did not worry the wealthy in the past; they were less aware, less informed than we are and felt less concern. It is only now, in our more knowing, more conscientious time, that we think about life's strange disparities. Our modern societies are the first, anywhere on earth, to *try* to provide enough for everybody. That, at least, is one great credit to the century of the common man.

How do we know anything about our ancestors? What they bought and how they organized their trade and their financial affairs? Wealth and social position had much more influence in the past than now; fine things were available for wealthy people and almost the only records of buying and selling are in the household account books, the bills, inventories, letters, and diaries of the well-to-do. Of merchants we catch only occasional glimpses through their legal transactions, their bankruptcy inventories, their punishments for fraud and their dealings with landlords and the Church.

Pictorial evidence is more vivid than any writing, but the belongings shown alongside their owners in paintings, drawings, and photographs were not all bought. People inevitably accumulated their possessions by generations of gifts and bequests and even the wealthy only purchased more when they needed to do so. So an eighteenth-century nobleman may have by his side in a portrait, a treasured possession acquired by an ancestor, and we cannot necessarily assume it to be a contemporary purchase. But as shops and markets developed and trade prospered, artists sometimes chose to depict people actually buying and selling, and such occasional social comment is revealing and mirrors the taste and economic status of the time.

There is too little in this book about poor people, but that is surely one of the facts of history. In all periods, in all parts of the world, most people have been poor, ignorant, illiterate, and insignificant. Ordinary men and women could rarely read or write, had little spare time in which to do so if they could, and anyway their incomes were so small that they had no need to keep a record of what they spent. They grew and made most of what they needed and bartered anything left over; clinging precariously to the rim of society, they were fortunate to survive at all.

How accurate can we hope to be in visualizing the past? We can never be sure, for it is indeed past – gone. Money values were entirely different from those of our own time and personal and social priorities, too, were poles apart from ours. New ideas could spread only slowly, goods were relatively more durable than they are today and, once settled, people did not move about as often as they do now, and so did not much need to re-equip their homes. Everybody's horizons were narrower and we are too far from them to guess whether 'this made for happiness and harmony or not.

Honesty and fair dealing in buying and selling were no

1 Covent Garden in the early nineteenth century. This famous London market grew up on the site of the gardens of wealthy houses on the Strand

greater or less in the past than they are nowadays. There have always been rogues, just as there have always been a majority of honest and hard-working citizens. What *was* very different in the past was the size of society, the scale of financial operations, the degree of control exercised by the authorities and the punishments meted out to those who cheated.

A curiously continuing factor is the extent to which potential customers have withheld from purchasing for moral and ethical reasons. The rebels in the American colonies boycotted English goods from time to time, just as many people, nowadays, refuse to buy or cannot obtain certain things for this or that social or political reason. Trade has always been a potential weapon. When I needed a certain scarf in the 1930s and refused to buy it because it turned out to have been made in the Japan that had recently attacked Manchuria, I felt I had made a significant gesture. Today, I may stop in the market to weigh up my responsibility before I buy South African apples, Israeli oranges, Russian tunny fish, or peaches flown in from Florida – but I may well feel foolish on returning home and unsure what it is that constitutes an ethical criterion of buying.

2 An American butcher's shop, about 1840. The lady is being given individual attention

3 A modern supermarket. Here the housewife is choosing her own meat

Individual logic appears to play little part in this; what we do arises largely as a result of spontaneous reaction to particular events and rational criteria have been overcome by the emotions of the moment. On a world scale, however, we are so inter-dependent that buying habits in any one country can have serious political repercussions elsewhere.

Human nature has changed little, and at a time when too many people look backwards to imaginary 'good old days', it is perhaps interesting, and it may even be useful, to glance at the shopping customs of our ancestors and to see how little, except in scale, our customs have changed. But shopping is now simpler than it has ever been before. On the whole we know where to go for what we want; we can, if we wish, be well informed as to what is available; the work of food and drug analysts, weights and measures inspectors, and many other public officials gives support to our buying; and we can buy goods from virtually every part of the world. Whereas our ancestors had to cope with problems of scarcity, we are faced with those of multiple choice.

One thing that is certain is that, throughout history, women – and many men too – have on the whole *enjoyed* their shopping. At times exciting, at times frustrating and difficult, buying and selling have always been lively social occasions – a traffic between people. The foremost character in Arthur Miller's play *The Price*, had this to say:

> What is the key word today? Disposable. The more you can throw it away the more it's beautiful. The car, the furniture, the wife, the children – everything has to be disposable. Because you see the main thing today is – shopping. Years ago a person, if he was unhappy, didn't know what to do with himself – he'd go to church, start a revolution – *something*. Today you're unhappy? Can't figure it out? What is the salvation? Go shopping.[1]

But time and ecological thinking move on. Since 1964, when this was written, we are now facing the problems of shortages and our future may well be less affluent than we once thought.

[1] Copyright © 1968 by Arthur Miller and Ingeborg M. Miller, trustee

9

2 *Before 1500*

IN THE MIDDLE AGES nearly everybody lived in the country and earned their living in some way from the land. Families were largely self-sufficient: they grew, reared, or caught their own food; they often sheared their own sheep, for wool which the women spun and wove into cloth; their leather, their tallow, their timber for building and for fuel were all available nearby. On the whole only local materials were available and even such things as earthenware, ploughs, and other farm tools were often made locally.

There was little need for money. The ambitious peasant or villein dreamed not of amassing a hoard of coins in his chest, but of acquiring more land to plough, more animals to rear, and more children in his family to help him in his labour. People then were probably no less interested in worldly goods than we are, but their horizons were limited to basic essentials; the things that money could buy were few and opportunity for self-advancement minimal.

Wealthy noblemen and churchmen also depended upon the land for their living, owning huge estates which provided their needs and taxing, both in money and in kind, those who worked for them. The work done by a villein for his lord was of two kinds: 'week-work' was done every week and varied in quantity from manor to manor; 'boon-work' was needed only at harvest time or any other such season of special effort. The villein kept himself during week-work, but it was usual for the lord to provide at least some food and drink while boon-work was being done. Later, a lord would sometimes allow his villeins to pay money instead of doing work for him, and thus buy a measure of freedom.

So the countryman sold any surplus he had in the local market, where he also bought, if he could, anything that he was not able to make for himself. Bread, meat, ale, firewood, candles, and goods made of wood, metal, leather, and cloth were the main commodities exchanged at the market.

From earliest times the countrymen who brought their produce to be sold in a town had to pay dues to the king or to the local lord. These dues gave them the right to enter the town,

4   Twelfth-century merchants displaying their goods.
Notice the laden pack horse and mule

the right to rent and set up a stall, called 'stallage', and to trade
in a certain fixed spot where potential buyers would know
where to find them. Doomsday Book mentions markets in about
fifty towns, and in the following centuries, as the population
increased and new towns were settled, the right to hold a
market was granted in more and more places.

A market could not be set up without permission and this
was refused if there was one already in the neighbourhood. A
famous thirteenth-century lawyer proclaimed that the distance
between markets should not be less than 6 miles, allowing time
for the walk to market in the early morning, the sale and
purchase of goods during the middle of the day, and a safe
return home before darkness fell. This latter was an important
consideration during a time of frequent robberies.

Once a market was established, the right of the town to hold
it could not be taken away, nor its day changed, except for very
serious reasons. Sunday marketing was forbidden in most
towns, even before the Norman Conquest, just as it is today,
but the law was frequently disregarded, since Sunday was a
convenient day for those who worked during the rest of the
week. Finally, in 1448, King Henry VI forbade the holding of

markets or fairs on Sundays; no goods were to be displayed on that day, 'necessary victual only except' – and none were to be sold in churchyards.

Those who were permitted to trade in the market had to keep to their allotted place, and not trade wherever they wished. A list of the stalls in the provision market at Norwich in 1397 shows forty butchers' stalls together, forty-five fishmongers' and twenty-eight poulterers', of which nine were used for fresh fish.

Trading hours were restricted, so that everyone might have an equal chance to buy a fair share of whatever was available. Buying before the market was open was a serious offence. At the market at Yarmouth nobody was permitted to 'open either sak, pooke . . . or any other vessell wherein victualls or other things be' until the market bell had rung.

'Cheap' was an Anglo-Saxon word meaning 'barter' or 'price'. A 'cheapman' or 'chapman' was a merchant who sold goods at market, and a travelling salesman was sometimes called a 'cheap-jack'. 'Chipping' was a derivation which meant 'selling' – as in Chipping Norton, Chipping Sodbury.

Special market regulations were made in certain towns. The city of Winchester possesses a parchment roll written in the fourteenth century, entitled 'These ben the olde usages of the Citie of Wynchestre, that haveth be – used in the tyme of oure elderne'. Many of the 'usages' are market regulations laying down the customs to be paid on each kind of goods, the times when the market could be kept, and what tolls were to be taken at the town gates for every cart-load or horse-load of goods entering. In Worcester, a busy town of weavers, part of the market was held in the 'yelde-hall' where the Town Council met to arrange the affairs of the city, and a loud bell was rung to warn people of the hours during which certain business might be transacted.

Market crosses were built to remind traders of the importance of honest dealing, according to the Faith, and became the places where tolls were paid. Later, when markets were covered in, the crosses were often placed on the roof of Buttermarkets, Yarnmarkets, and Market Halls. These, in places, became Town Halls or Guild Halls.

Wherever men and women gather together for buying and selling, disputes are sure to arise. Even today, Inspectors of

Food and Drugs and of Weights and Measures are accepted as essential to fair trading, and in medieval times the need for control was no less great. In every market there was a court composed of local merchants, held by the mayor in the Tollbooth or some other central place in the town. This was the 'Court of Pie Powder', or 'Pieds Poudrés' – dusty feet. It was so-called because the litigants came straight into the court from the street to make their complaints and to have their differences settled. Offenders were punished immediately.

5   An early dispensary. Apprentices are grinding and blending the drugs

Many attempts were made by enterprising or unscrupulous traders to 'forestall' by buying in advance before goods reached the market and to 'regrate' or hold up supplies to create a scarcity. In Norwich, in the thirteenth century, it was reported that

> The wife of Henry Lant is wont to buy fowls, hens, capons and other things in the market on Saturdays and sell them on Sundays at the gates of the Holy Trinity, to great heightening and forestalling, and is a common forestaller, whereof great outcry has arisen.

6 A countinghouse scene from the fourteenth century.
Notice the clerk writing the accounts

And in the same city there is record of an innkeeper, John de
Gaywood, who, in 1374,

> forestalled so many eggs in the market that he filled twenty-eight
> barrels at divers times and sent them out of the kingdom to foreign
> parts, and likewise forestalled butter and cheese to large amount .

Such practices were illegal, but the fact that the regulations
were frequently repeated shows that they were disobeyed and
that there were plenty of people willing to risk a fine or punishment in order to make a profit.

It was, however, a great medieval principle that profit should
not accrue without cause. Private enterprise was considered
selfish and wrong and it was generally accepted that traders and
craftsmen should be content with a reasonable profit and not
take unfair advantage of the needs of their neighbours. For
instance, in London in 1362, when tiles were in great demand
because of damage caused by a very fierce storm, the tilers were
ordered to go on making tiles and selling them at the usual
prices.

The regulation of 'scot and lot' decreed that anybody buying
goods at a bargain price was obliged to share the advantage

with others, allowing them to buy from him at the price he had paid, and keeping only his fair portion.

Food prices were strictly controlled by town officials. Their regular meeting to control the sale of bread and ale – basic diet in all parts of the country – was called the Assize. It fixed the amount of bread in a loaf and the strength of ale in a gallon, but not the actual money cost. This was because there were very limited coins in existence and change could rarely be given. The chief coin was the silver penny, which was sometimes marked with a cross so that it could be broken into four quarters, or 'Farthings'. For centuries one loaf or one quart of ale cost two farthings; the ale would be weaker and the loaf smaller after a bad season when barley and wheat were dear.

There were different kinds of bread – wastel, or second quality; pouf, or puffe bread; and demesne or Panis Dominicus, made of the very finest flour and having a figure of our Lord stamped on it. Troute, or trete bread was the very coarsest brown; horse-bread was a coarse kind made of peas and beans. In towns it was common for dough to be made at home and taken to the baker's to be baked with his own loaves; in a village too small to have a baker the only oven existing would probably belong to the lord of the manor, who made a profit out of those who used it, as he did from allowing the villagers to use his mill for grinding corn.

The Assize of Bread and Ale was treated very seriously but the records of most medieval towns are full of complaints about dishonest brewers and bakers and of the punishments meted out to them. In Chester when, after a bad harvest, the price of wheat rose to 46s a quarter, the mayor and council fixed the weight of a half-penny loaf at $6\frac{1}{2}$ ounces. The bakers refused to bake loaves of this size, even when the officials carefully reconsidered their complaint and decided that the charge was indeed 'laufull, necessary and suffycyent for the bayker to lyve upon'. Bread became very scarce and the mayor instructed everybody to provide for themselves as much as possible and then authorized anyone to bake good bread and bring it to market, in which case they should '. . . have redy monye for ther bred and hartye thankes'. It is interesting to note that the bakers finally submitted to the mayor's decision and were allowed to work again after payment of fines.

Other foodstuffs sold in markets were usually free of any

price control, except in a crisis. Much of the meat eaten was not bought at market because virtually all families kept animals of their own, even in towns. Large households bought their meat – if they bought it at all – 'on the hoof' and killed it themselves, so that they could use the tallow for making candles and the hide for leather.

But food traders of all kinds tried restrictive practices from time to time and when the butchers of Chester found that 'foreign' (ie country) butchers had been admitted into the city, they refused to kill any meat. The mayor acted firmly, committing the lot of them to prison and they were only released as a concession, when they submitted to his order,

> . . . consideringe allsoe the lamentable waylinge and humble sub-mission of the said company, their great charge of wives and children, their imbesilitie and wekeness, and the danger of the tyme, being very fervent hott wether, the company many in number, and the straitness [restriction] of rome in the said gaole.

In the fourteenth-century records of Winchester, rules were laid down about the sale of fish and poultry – they were not to be bought wholesale before 9 o'clock in the morning, a board on which fish was shown for sale paid rent of a farthing a day, every cart-load of fish paid a halfpenny, butchers paid for their stalls and merchants of unslaughtered goats, sheep, and swine were registered. Bakers must offer good bread of full weight, those from outside who sold their bread in the High Street had to pay more rent than those standing in the other streets, and every baker must put his seal upon his loaves. Here, and else-where in many other towns, rules for the sale of food supplies in market were carefully made to hinder anyone who would take advantage of the public's needs, and to ensure fair dealing for everybody.

Prices of other goods were also controlled from time to time. Among the proclamations and regulations of the Corporation of Bristol during the fourteenth century 'It is ordained that the tailors of the town shall not in future take for the cutting and making of a robe more than 18d, under penalty of 40d, [and] that the aforesaid tailors shall find thread, buckram, and silk for the lining of the sleeves' and 'That no man who is a master of the said craft [the Fullers, who fulled, or beat worsted cloth as it came from the loom, to make it more durable] shall pay to any stallager [workman] but 6d a day as well in summer as in winter, and no more. And if it be found that any master pay more, that he pay to the commanalty 5s.'

Every trade was regulated by its Guild, which controlled prices and standards of work. The Guild's officers regularly and carefully inspected the work of members, because dishonest workmen could give a trade a bad name.

In 1346 the Guild of Weavers of Bristol instructed: 'If the threads are thin in the cloth, or are too far apart, the cloth and the instrument on which it is worked ought to be burnt' and the regulations of the Guild of Pepperers of London in 1316 give us an interesting insight into the kinds of cheating which went on:

> That no one of the trade . . . shall mix any manner of wares, that is to say, shall put old things with new, or new things with old . . . nor yet things of one price, or of one sort, with things of another price, or of another sort. Also that no one shall moisten any manner of merchandise, such as saffron, alum, ginger, cloves, and such manner of things as admit of being moistened; that is to say, by steeping the ginger or turning the saffron out of the sack and then anointing it, or bathing it in water; by reason whereof any manner of weight may be increased, or any deterioration arise to the merchandise.

7 A mason and carpenter are being inspected by an officer to see that they maintain the high standards of their Guild

There were other ingenious ways of cheating customers. Bakers put weights into loaves or, while making up their customers' own dough, stole a portion of it by means of a little trap door in the kneading board and a boy sitting crouched under the counter. Complaints were made in 1472 about frauds in the upholstery trade: in such articles as feather-beds, cushions, and quilts, the buyer 'seeth withoute and knoweth not the stuff within'; down pillows were sometimes 'stuffed with thistill downe and cattes tailles' and 'materas stuffed with here and flokkes and sold for flokkes'. Cloth was sometimes stretched before being sold, or carefully folded to hide defects; a length of bad cloth might be joined on to a length of better quality; inferior leather was cleaned up to look like the best; pots and pans might be made of poor quality metal which melted when put on the fire, and so on. In Norwich a butcher secretly bought eight drowned sheep and sold the carcasses as good mutton, and in the same town a fishwife mixed herrings with a barrel of oysters and sold it 'to strangers'.

8   A fifteenth-century wine-gauger, or exciseman testing the quantity and quality of imported wine

9 A draper's shop about 1500. The apprentices are measuring the cloth

All trading offences were punished in public in stocks or pillory. Justice was seen to be done, it was done quickly, and the punishment did, indeed 'fit the crime'. Local officials had continually to be looking out for trouble but sometimes they relented: one Richard Lewes had been selling brown bread unfit even for horses to eat and was condemned to be drawn on a hurdle through the town. His punishment was remitted on the grounds that he was an old man and that it was winter-time. In the records of the Guildhall, in London, there is reference to a woman condemned to the pillory for selling a penny bun underweight.

In London, in 1364, one John Penrose '. . . sold red wine to all who came there, unsound and unwholesome for man'. The judgement was 'that the said John Penrose shall drink a draught of the same wine which he sold to the common people; and the remainder of such wine shall then be poured on the head of the same John; and that he shall forswear the calling [occupation] of a vintner in the city of London for ever, unless he can obtain the favour of our lord the king as to the same.'

And here is what happened to a baker's servant who tried to trick customers:

> Robert Porter, servant of John Gibbe, baker of Stratforde, was brought here, into the Guildhall of London, before Nicholas Extone, Mayor of the said city, John Hadle, and other Aldermen, and questioned for that, when the same Mayor on that day went into Chepe, to make assay there of bread, according to the custom of the City, he, the said Robert, knowing that the bread of his master, in a certain cart there, was not of full weight, took a penny loaf, and in it falsely and fraudulently inserted a piece of iron, weighing 6s 8d [ie about one third of a pound], with intent to make the said loaf weigh more, in deceit of the people . . .
>
> Wherefore, enquiry was made of the same Robert, how he would acquit himself thereof; upon which, he acknowledged that he had done in manner aforesaid. And for his said falsity and deceit, it was adjudged that he should be taken from thence to Cornhulle, and be put upon the pillory there, to remain upon the same for one hour of the day, the said loaf and piece of iron being hung about his neck. And precept was given to the Sheriffs, to have the reason for such punishment publicly proclaimed.

In London strict regulation of the meat trade was enforced in the late Middle Ages when more people were able to buy meat and there were problems about the disposal of offal. Public feeling was strongly against throwing stinking rubbish into public sewers and butchers had to organize special shambles (abbatoirs), for instance at Queenhithe, where rubbish had to be rowed into mid-stream and dumped at ebb-tide. In 1402, a pier was built off Pudding Lane for the Eastcheap butchers' convenience.

Town officials made their own regulations about the opening of shops, to suit local needs. In Bristol for instance shoemakers were allowed at any time and even on Sundays, to serve 'eny knyght or Squyer or eny other straunger goyng on her passage or journee, or merchant or maryner comyng from the see' and also, during the six Sundays of harvest, anyone else who required boots.

There were stringent rules against working at night or after dark in all kinds of trades, 'by reason that no man can work so neatly by night as by day'. The customer was to be protected against the shoddy work that could so easily be overlooked by candle-light. All secret trading was thought to be suspicious and there were frequent regulations against it: at Bristol, for example, weavers had to work at looms visible from the street and not in cellars or upstairs rooms. Such trade regulations seem to us to be very confusing but all had good local cause.

Apart from its regular and eventful market days, a town in the Middle Ages was a collection of craftsmen and their families and not, as now, a collection of shopkeepers. Most goods were sold by the men and women who made them. As well as sellers of more everyday requirements, the bowyers cut the bows and the fletchers made the arrows used by the archers, and they sold them at the front of their workshops. The armourer forged the armour needed by knights, the goldsmith beat out gold into cups and brooches, the tanner prepared the skins which the shoemaker next door made into shoes, the potter's wheel could be seen from the street, and each craftsman stopped his work to serve his customers.

The man we call a shopkeeper, who buys goods to sell again, had very little place in early medieval society. He was disliked and mistrusted and town authorities did all they could to prevent him from operating in their area. A craftsman had a booth outside the door of his house, on which he displayed some of his goods while others hung from his windows. At night everything was stored in the cellar. A large sign hung outside each house; these had to be at least 9 feet above the level of the street, to allow a man on horseback to ride underneath in safety. There were no pavements and customers stood in the mud and filth which inevitably collected in every street.

A good deal of marketing was carried out by pedlars who carried packs of mixed goods, and wandered from town to town. There was much opposition to these 'evechepynges' as they were called, because they often cheated and were the cause of general disorder. In London they were such a nuisance that in 1347 a large committee of citizens was appointed to see that they were kept out of the highway of Cheap.

Haberdashers were in a different category from the pedlars, but they served the same purpose of linking specialist craftsmen and the public. They were an organized body of shopkeepers who made nothing themselves, but kept a varied stock of merchandise. Various contemporary accounts indicate that their largest single line consisted of coarse woollen caps worn by the working people, but they also sold girdles, purses, buttons, babies' boots, bells, straps, spurs, chains, bow-strings, dishes, boxes, paper, linen thread, plaster images, beads, ivory combs, gaming-tables, and spectacles. A modern haberdasher's stock is somewhat less varied than this, but we can see that their traditional mixture of goods is very old.

Grocers were merchants who carried out business in bulk – *en gros* – and in London the Grocers' Company developed by the amalgamation of spicers, pepperers, corders trading largely in canvas, and apothecaries. The link between the canvas-dealers and the others is obscure, but perhaps they sold canvas containers for carrying the other goods.

Gradually, buying and selling became more and more separated from *making*. The overall concern of the mayor and aldermen of a city was to ensure that there were sufficient goods for the needs of the public. The wish of an enterprising trader to extend his range of goods inevitably often clashed with the wish of others to keep their monopolies.

Some of the minor crafts showed remarkable instances of specialization. For instance, there was a distinction between the makers of white and brown bread, between workers in new leather, called cordwainers, and those in old leather, called cobblers. Such lines of demarcation were drawn in the interests of the customers, to make sure that sound materials were used, by men who understood their craft.

Money-lending was freely practised in the Middle Ages among the poor as well as the rich. Usury was forbidden by law, but there were all kinds of subtle devices for hiding usurious transactions. Sometimes for example, the lender might note down as lent, more money than was really paid, so that when the debt was settled the borrower knowingly paid more than he had originally received and so the lender got his interest.

We, nowadays, are accustomed to know what kind of shop or market to go to for what we need. Shopping in the Middle Ages must have been much more of a hit and miss affair, and the housewife had to find what she could where she could. There are records of armourers selling wine; of a glover selling silk purses and painted cloths as well as gloves; and merchants in Kingston are recorded as buying and selling, in the same shop, fish, wine, fruit, beer, butter, honey, soap, dye, horse-shoes, bonnets, linen cloth, and thread.

The bankruptcy records of a mercer in Leicester tell us of the goods that could be bought from him:

[He] was at the same time draper, haberdasher, jeweller, grocer, ironmonger, saddler, and dealer in timber, furniture and hard-ware. Even this does not describe him adequately, for he had a small stock of wool, wool-fells and skins on hand, and he could have offered you ready-made gowns in taffeta or silk, daggers, bowstrings, harpstrings, writing-paper, materials for making ink, and seeds for the vegetable garden. His resources were greatest in the drapery department, which comprised twenty different kinds of British and imported cloth; he was also well stocked with small wares, notably purses of gold cloth, belts, ribbons, skeins of Paris silk, children's stockings, silk coifs, and kerchiefs for nuns. In the way of hardware he had everything from cutlery and candelabra to coal-skuttles and horse-shoes.[1]

The lease of a draper's house and shop in the parish of St Christopher in London, where the Bank of England now stands, describes a home of middling comfort:

In the shop there were two couch-boards (to hold the goods) and a showing-board (or counter) and the shop was hung with black buckram, 'stained' or painted with some ornament. In the window there was a stall for the display of goods, and in the adjoining warehouse there were more couch-boards. For living rooms there was a hall ceiled with estrich board (deal from East Europe), opening out of the kitchen. The kitchen was paved, and had a lead cistern, a dressing board, two shelves and a hatch. There was also a buttery. Upstairs there seem to have been three chambers; in one there was a standing bed, in another a press covered with boards round about and closed underneath.[2]

Even if one knew where to shop for what one wanted, and even if the particular traders were honest, buying and selling in the Middle Ages must have been very confusing, for weights and measures were vague to a degree that seems impossible to our more orthodox and regulated customs, and they varied between one district, one town, and another. Some purchases were not weighed or measured at all: there is frequent reference

[1] *Studies in English Trade in the 15th century*, Power and Postan, Routledge 1933
[2] *Prejudice and Promise in Fifteenth Century England*, Kingsford, The Ford Lectures 1923-4

10 Merchants shipping their goods down the Rhein, 1484. Commercial centres grew up on rivers as they meant quick and easy transport to other countries

to buying such items as 'a salmon as thick as a man's arm', as much hay 'as a man can lift', as much wood 'as a man may bear', cloth 'two ells wide between the fists',[1] and so on. London drapers bought cloth by the 'yard and a hand'; though this was forbidden, 'the yarde and handful' was known as a London measure as late as the end of the sixteenth century. Coal was sold by the 'seam' (or horse-load), the 'load', 'corf', or 'perch' in Warwickshire, and on Tyneside by the 'fother', 'chauldron', and 'keep' or barge-load.

Medieval people had a craving for spices, because of the great emphasis upon preserving meat and fish. Their recipes are full of strong, hot ingredients though it may well be that we have an exaggerated impression of the spiciness of medieval food. It is more than likely that problems of transport and storage may have affected the strength of many imported spices. Most weaken in flavour fairly soon and probably a great quantity was needed in order to achieve a moderate flavour.

[1] The standard of the ell, which is virtually the modern yard, was established in Henry I's reign, and according to William of Malmesbury, was the length of the King's arm.

Pepper was one of the most expensive articles and it is interesting to note that in the north of England even this basic spice was imported only in tiny lots worth a few shillings each and not by the bale[1] as in London. When the Venerable Bede, Bishop of Durham, lay dying, he distributed his few belongings among his brethren, and divided a little parcel of pepper as one of his most valued possessions.

Until the thirteenth century standard measures were often fixed by declaring a particular vessel to *be* the standard, and then copies of the vessel could be made and bought. We do not know the sizes or the shapes of these measures, as none of them have survived, but it is likely that people bought dry goods from a large, wide vessel, and liquids from a narrower, smaller one.

Standards were fixed by royal decree time and time again, but most towns had their own measures and attempts to bring some order into the system failed frequently. For example, at Bury St Edmunds the town council tried to introduce the use of London weights and measures, but as a result trade was paralysed. Nobody brought any more goods to the market, preferring to carry them to other towns where trade was still in the measures with which they were familiar.

In 1215 Magna Carta declared 'there shall be one measure

[1] Hence, perhaps, the link with the canvas-makers in London?

11 Pepper was a valuable spice. Here merchants are testing the quality of the harvest before they buy; Malabar, twelfth century

of wine throughout our realm, and one measure of ale, and one measure of corn, namely the London quarter . . .'

This has often been taken to mean that there should be three *different* measures for wine, ale, and corn, but it is doubtful whether this was really the intention, for it would merely have complicated an already involved issue. Magna Carta was drawn up in a great hurry, so this particular clause may well have been intended only to ensure that 'something would be done' about weights and measures (a Statement of Intent, in the modern phrase). In fact nothing was done until a century later and, even then, things do not seem to have been made very clear. The *Tractatus de Ponderibus et Mensuris* which became law early in the fourteenth century stated:

> An English penny . . . shall weigh 32 wheat grains from the middle of the ear, and an ounce shall weigh 20 pence. And 12 ounces make a London pound . . . and 8 pounds make a gallon of wine, and 8 gallons of wine make a London bushel.

Local variations continued in spite of such laws, and customs became more and more complicated and confused until Parliament, in 1491, petitioned the king to issue new standard measures, and this was done. At this time town authorities hired out weighing and measuring devices to traders at considerable profit and only gradually could they possess their own. These had, of course, to be frequently inspected to prevent fraud, as is still the case today.

In the earlier Middle Ages the wealth of England consisted mainly in raw products and there was very little industry. In the fifteenth century 'manufacturing' was developing in nearly every town, and the most important of all was the manufacture of cloth.

In 1352 the Commons told the king that raw wool was 'La Soveraine Marchandise and Jewel' of England. A hundred years later they declared that 'the makeyng of cloth' was the 'grettest occupacion and lyving' of the poor people of the land.

The expansion of trade and rising expectations among most classes of people led to increasing production and a new class of men arose who had enough capital to finance new industries. In the cloth industry these men were called clothiers; they employed carders, spinners, dyers, fullers, and weavers, and when the cloth was made they sold it to drapers, who gradually became exclusively dealers in cloth.

12   In this illustration from a fourteenth-century French manuscript, shop keepers display their goods. Notice the pharmacist (*bottom right*) selling tonic wine, and behind him, (*centre*) the leech

There is frequent mention of cloth-making in government regulations during the late Middle Ages and an extraordinary number of different kinds of material are mentioned. The housewife who could afford to do so could choose from more than a dozen different varieties of worsteds and cloths with such mysterious but inviting names as vervise, plounkett, turkyne, celestines, carsey, vesses, pacykng whites, brode cloth, bastardes, kendales, friseware fustian, says and serges, and stamyns and mustrevalers!

A great deal of the European commerce of the Middle Ages was transacted at fairs. The word originated from the Latin 'feria' or holiday, and it is likely that some British fairs were established during the Roman occupation and added to during the Anglo-Saxon period. The Normans encouraged fairs in the interest of the Church and most early fairs were associated with religious ceremonies and held on the feast days of local saints. At Bromsgrove, for example, the fair was on Midsummer Day, the feast of St John the Baptist, at Rothwell on Trinity Sunday eve; in both instances, and many others, the church was dedicated to the saint whose day was thus celebrated. At Ely the fair gave a new word to our language: the fair was in honour of St Audrey, a woman who believed that, in early life, she had sinned in wearing fine clothes and rich jewellery. Her influence caused local women to want to wear cheap necklaces of lace in place of jewels, and in time the phrase 'St Audrey's lace' became corrupted to 'tawdry lace' and the adjective came to mean cheap and inferior.

A market drew people from the neighbourhood, but an annual fair gave opportunities to merchants travelling from a distance and even from other countries. The biggest fairs were virtually international markets and merchants bought bales of English wool in exchange for all manner of luxuries: silks and velvets from Italy, wines from France, furs from the Baltic, exotic spices, fruits and perfumes from the Levant, woad from Toulouse, the best iron from Spain, madder and brass ware from the Low Countries and the Rhineland, and fine porcelain from the Orient. Everyone, layman and cleric alike, bought at the fair.

In the fourteenth century the fair at Winchester lasted for twenty-four days and, since the year 1079 when the Bishop had secured the grant of a fair from William Rufus, the revenues had been spent upon building and repairing the great Norman Cathedral there, and St Swithin's Priory nearby. The fair itself was virtually a wooden town, covering the whole space of a hill near the city. It was surrounded by a palisade with only one gate, as a defence against thieves and to prevent traders from bringing goods to the fair without paying the required tolls.

Here is a proclamation concerning the opening of another important medieval fair, that of St Bartholomew in London:

> . . . That no manner of persons make any congregation . . . or affrays by which the . . . peace may be broken or disturbed. Also that all manner of sellers of wine, ale or beer, sell by measures ensealed, as by gallon, pottle, quart, and pint. And that no person sell any bread, but if it keep the assize, and that it be good and wholesome for man's body. And that no manner of cook, pie-baker, nor huckster, sell nor put to sale any manner of victual, but that it be good and wholesome for man's body. And that no manner of person buy nor sell, but with true weights and

measures, sealed according to the statute in that behalf made. And that no manner of person . . . whatever, within the limits and bounds of this fair, presume to break the Lord's Day in selling . . . or in buying . . . any commodities whatsoever, or in sitting, tippling or in drinking in any tavern, inn, ale-house, tippling-house or cook's house . . . and finally that what persons soever find themselves grieved, injured, or wronged by any manner of person in this fair, that they come with their plaints, before the stewards in their fair . . . and they will minister to all parties justice, according to the laws of this land and the customs of this city.

Roads were very bad in medieval England, and they remained so for another three or four centuries. But carriers nevertheless went regularly from town to town and were employed for conveying goods, letters, and valuables. In the Paston letters we read that the carrier from Norwich took four days to reach London. In November 1474 he was paid '40d to pay for the third hired horse, and he bringeth three horses with him'. Chapmen, too, made their regular rounds and by these means much of the inland trade of the country was carried out. Goods were also sent by river: barges plied regularly on the Thames and took four days from London to Henley, where they frequently delivered wine, fish, and house-hold stores to the Stonor family living nearby.

There are frequent references to robbery on the roads, and of course there was no kind of insurance of goods or persons. William Marchall, a clerk in London, had property in Oxford-shire. His local agent was one Thomas Makyn who wrote often to him on business matters. One letter, asking for payment of 40s, he sent by the Oxford carrier whom he evidently did not trust, for he advised Marchall to hide the money: 'Buy a pound of powdered pepper to carry the money privily or else two pounds of rice, for that makes great bulk.' We do not know whether this simple ruse was successful or not.

By the later Middle Ages most people of any position seem to have been literate. The wives and sisters of country gentlemen could often write as well as their husbands and brothers, and both they and many of their servants could keep regular household accounts. Many shopkeepers made out bills in writing to the Stonor family in Oxfordshire. When Lady Stonor wanted 38 yards of satin known as 'sarcenet', at 5s a yard, the merchant wrote as follows:

13 Fifteenth-century shops in a covered market. One merchant is selling shoes, another cloth, and the man on the right is a goldsmith

Madam, the sarcenet is very fine. I think most profitable and most worshipful for you, and shall last you your life and your child's after you, whereas harlotry of 3s 4d or 3s 5d a yard would not ensure two seasons with you. Therefore, for a little more cost, me thinketh most wisdom to take of the best . . .

Many of us would consider the merchant's principle still very sound, but who, today, could begin to think of fabric which might last for two generations!

Very many clothes were passed on in that way, but children and servants were usually dressed in 'homespun' cloth, of a rough, loose texture, such as Piers Plowman described: 'unless a louse could have leapt a little she could never have walked on so thread-bare a weave'.

One difficulty about laying in stores at the fair, for a house-keeper of Lady Stonor's position, was that she would be expected to pay cash, but in an age of self-sufficiency and occasional barter ready money was often scarce. Sir William Stonor was a large landowner, a Member of Parliament, and a Sheriff of the County, but he was constantly in debt to his tradesmen. His Steward wrote to him about these matters:

> . . . furthermore, sir, your mastership shall understand that the ale-brewer calls on me daily sore for money, the which I have written unto your mastership aforetime. The sum is £5 and odd money, the which he beseeches your mastership he may have some money in hand . . . Also, sir I beseech your mastership that you will remember your bread baker, for he calls upon me daily for money, the which sum is 35s 3d.

We have very little idea of the quantities in which goods were bought in medieval England, but we do know that nothing was wrapped or packaged. It was the purchaser who provided the necessary containers—baskets, jugs, bowls, or sacks – and who drove home the pig he had bought or carried poultry dangling by the legs.

Neither do we know much about the amount of trading done at any particular fair or market. We do know about prices, for there are plenty of records of housekeeping expenditure, such as the Northumberland Household Book of 1512 and others earlier. What we cannot do is to compare the figures, the quantities, the decisions, and choices people made with those of our own time.

The whole framework was so different. As one writer has simply and clearly put it:

> Nobody takes home corn, or cartwheels, or iron bars from the shops today, but people did so then, to grind their own flour or make a cart with their own timber, or to hand over to the smith to make ploughshares. And it was the price of such things that was important to medieval people, rather than the prices of what we nowadays call 'consumer' goods.[1]

[1] *A History of Shopping*, Davis, Routledge 1966.

3 The Sixteenth Century

THE SIXTEENTH CENTURY in England was a busy and exciting time in which to live, a time of great change in manners, in social life and in material standards. Men's ideas were changing rapidly and so were their expectations. In the Middle Ages, everyone knew his place and very few people became much richer or poorer than their parents had been. Now, fortunes might be won and lost and power was moving from the aristocracy to the merchant class. Under the Tudors it was no longer birth, but money that made a gentleman.

Even the map of the world was changing, for countries were being discovered which had not been heard of before. Men were finding wealth and adventure in trading and fighting on distant shores, and the wealth and goods they brought home increased the prosperity of townsman and countryman alike.

In no other country, at this time, were more prodigious households maintained by the gentry than in England, and foreign visitors commented frequently upon the standards kept even in middle-class houses. But as there were no banks it was not always easy to know how to use extra money other than by investing it in household goods.

Not everyone welcomed the new opportunities or the new fashions which people began to buy for their houses and their clothing. William Harrison, Rector of Radwinter in Essex, and later Canon of Windsor, writing in *A Description of England* in 1587 complained:

> The fantastical folly of our nation (even from the courtier to the carter[1]) is such that no form of apparel liketh us longer than the first garment is in the wearing, if it continue so long, and be not laid aside to receive some other trinket newly devised by the fickle-headed tailors . . .

England was still overwhelmingly an agrarian community; the great mass of her population still lived by the land and the typical unit was the village, not the city. There was only one city, London, with a population (in 1545) of about 80,000. Other cities, such as Norwich, Bristol, and Exeter, were important trading centres in their areas, but would have

[1] Surely, a testy clerical over-statement!

seemed to us to be no more than small country towns. The towns that John Leland noted during his travels in the years 1535–43 were what we would call villages, for some had only a single street and the countryside extended right into the 'town'.

The narrow streets of Tudor towns, which look so charming to us in retrospect, must really have been very unpleasant. There was no traffic control; only very feeble light was provided by the lanterns which innkeepers and the wealthier inhabitants were ordered to hang out; and piles of rubbish were left outside every house and shop. The bye-laws of the manor of Bishops Hall in Chelmsford in 1664 included many references to uncleanliness in the town, some of which referred to shopkeepers:

> Item, that neither the butcher nor any person at any time hereafter shall cast any horns, bones, or any other filth in the street or in the river there, penalty 3s 4d.

But sixteenth-century noses were a good deal less sensitive than ours and there must have been a great deal of interest and enjoyment in listening to shopkeepers and apprentices shouting outside their premises, trying to entice customers to buy:

> . . . Will ye buy a very fine cabinet, a fine scarf, or a rich girdle and hangers? See here, madam, fine cobweb lawn, good cambric, or fair bone lace. Will ye buy any very fine silk stocks sir? See here a fair hat of the French block sir. What do ye lack, do ye buy sir, see what ye lack? Pins, points, garters, Spanish gloves, or silk ribbons?

The term 'merchant' in sixteenth-century England covered a very wide range of wealth, activity, and respectability, from the rich London businessman to struggling provincial shopkeepers, from crooks to gentlemen.

Many Tudor merchants lived in tall 'black-and-white' houses such as we can still see at Chester, Shrewsbury, and Exeter; others in solid stone or timber-framed houses. Wherever they were, these houses were a great deal larger than their narrow frontage suggests. There was a shop on the street level in front, and kitchen and service rooms extended behind. On the first floor was the hall or living room, running back from the street, and on the higher floors were the bedrooms. Such houses were often three or four stories high and the richer merchants would have two or even three such dwellings built together to make an impressive home, richly carved along the front.

33

14 A pedlar with his tray of trinkets, 1516

The High Street of many a flourishing small town, with its buzzing market, contained imposing merchants' houses thickly surrounded by the shops of tailors, goldsmiths, drapers, saddlers, and others. In the early sixteenth century a Bristol widow, Alice Chester, who traded in cloth, rebuilt her house in the middle of the city, and fortunately her agreement with a Welsh carpenter, Stephen Morgan, is preserved among the archives of All Saints' Church in Bristol. We read that Stephen was to build it of good timber and boards, it was to be only 10 feet 5 inches wide, but nearly 20 feet in length from front to back. On the ground floor was to be a shop, over it a hall with an oriel window, above this a chamber, also with an oriel, and on the fourth floor another chamber. The lattice had to be made by another craftsman, so we can assume that the windows may have been leaded. Such a tall, narrow house would also have had one or more storeys below ground level, for the storage of merchandise.

The typical sixteenth-century shop consisted, as it had done in the Middle Ages, of a single room, with a large unglazed window, the shutter of which let down to form a counter. Some

15　An early drawing of Eastcheap market

goods were displayed in the window, and the shopkeepers'
wives and daughters often sat in their doorways to act as
additional attractions. There is a robust realism and enthusiasm
about such behaviour which strikes oddly on our present day
attitudes.

Many of the shops were still also the work-rooms where the
articles were made, but more and more imported goods were
being sold in London and an Elizabethan writer commented:

> I have heard within these forty years, when there were not of
> these haberdashers that selles French or Millen cappes, glasses,
> knives, daggers, swordes, gyrdles and such thinges, not a dosen in
> all London; now from the Tower to Westminster alonge, every
> streete is full of them, and their shoppes glytter and shyne of
> glasses, as well drynkyng as lookyng; yes all manner of vessel of
> the same stuffe; painted cruses, gay daggers, knyves, swords and
> gyrdels; that it is able to make any temperate man to gase on
> them and to buy somewhat, though it serve to no purpose
> necessarie.

The 'temperate man' of sixteenth-century London would

indeed 'gase' in astonishment if he could see the variety of unnecessary goods displayed four centuries later along those same streets!

A foreigner who visited London early in the century was impressed by the houses of the greater merchants, particularly by their gardens, and by the double row of houses built over the shops of mercers and haberdashers on London Bridge. All traders tended to congregate in certain districts, as they had done in the Middle Ages when the 'shops' were only market stalls: the grocers sold in Bucklersbury, the skinners in Budge Row, the tavern-keepers and cooks in Eastcheap (where Falstaff's inn, the Boar's Head, stood), the tallow-chandlers in Candlewick Street (later Cannon Street), and the goldsmiths in Cheapside.

John Stow, a sixteenth-century historian, described the merchants' houses in Goldsmiths' Row as:

> ... the most beautiful frame of houses and shops that be within the walls of London, or elsewhere ... ten fair dwelling houses and fourteen shops, all in one frame, uniformly builded four storeys high, beautified towards the street with the goldsmiths' arms cast in lead, richly painted over and gilt.

16   Spectacle makers in an Italian town

The actors' tavern, the Mermaid, was in Cheapside, and the booksellers' in St Paul's Churchyard. A number of good shops were arranged in the upper storeys of the new Royal Exchange, built by Sir Thomas Gresham in imitation of the Antwerp Bourse, but those on the ground floor did not do so well, for it was too dark. In the open courtyard of the Exchange the merchants met to discuss their business.

It had become the practice to use St Paul's Cathedral as, virtually, a market place. The nave was a sanctuary for debtors, and also a parade-ground for elegant men and women. Here pilgrims bought badges and souvenirs from rows of stalls; professional scribes were licensed to sit at tables in the west end of the church, where they wrote letters for illiterate customers and drew up legal documents. Here, too, the fashionable tailor took orders and measured his customers; the well-dressed man went to show off his new clothes, and in the Churchyard nearby he could buy the books he might want, printed by William Caxton of Westminister or by his apprentice Wynkyn de Worde, in his house in Fleet Street, hard by 'at the syne of the Sonne'.

From time to time the Dean of St Paul's protested about the many secular uses of the building and in 1554 the Common Council of London had to step in and forbid – among many other abuses – the leading of horses and mules through the building.

We should not think of Tudor society as static or immobile. Men of all classes moved frequently from one district to another throughout the century and flocked to London. Coaches were not in general use, but there were traffic problems in London, nonetheless, and at times shopping must have been very diffi-cult. Fynes Moryson in his *Itinerary* of 1607 wrote:

> Coaches are not to be hired anywhere but only in London, and the ways far from London are so dirty as hired coachmen do not ordinarily take any long journeys. Sixty or seventy years ago coaches were very rare in England, but at this day pride is so far increased as there be few gentlemen of any account who have not their coaches, so as the streets of London are almost stopped up with them.

Many noblemen were conspicuously extravagant and spent vast sums on building and maintaining great houses. Burghley, Audley End, Hardwick, Syon and many other fine mansions swallowed up enormous amounts of money for the purchase of fine furniture, tapestries, gold, and silver. Heavy expenditure on clothes was another important item, as we know from the £1,000 owed by the Earl of Arundel to various mercers and tailors.

Buying expensive clothes was a sound investment for a rising man hoping to make an impression at court. Garments could be sold and re-sold, repaired, re-trimmed, and turned, and new ones bought to keep up appearances. One of the characters in Ben Jonson's play *Every Man Out of His Humour* says:

> To be an accomplished gentleman you must give over house-keeping in the country and live altogether in the City among gallants, where at your first appearance t'were good you turned four or five acres of your best land into two or three trunks of apparell.

One sixteenth-century writer defined the different qualities of men and women in this way: '. . . the man stern, strong, bold, adventurous, negligent of beauty, and spending; the woman weak, fearful, fair, curious of her beauty'.

That the man was the chief spender in the sixteenth-century household we can readily believe when we look at the fine clothes in his portraits, the heavily decorated furniture he liked, and the fine gold and silver articles he collected to prove his social importance. He liked his women to be richly adorned too, but it was only very slowly that the feudal attitude began to change: 'The wife', as one writer put it with seeming approval, 'in her husband's lifetime has nothing of her own, nor can she make any purchase with her own money.'

There was a great deal of sham in Elizabethan society. Sir John Harrington, the Queen's favourite godson, wrote of the weaknesses of the time:

> We go brave in apparel that we may be taken for better men than we be, we use much bombastings and quiltings to seem better framed, better shouldered, smaller waisted, and fuller thighed than we are, we barb and shave oft to seem younger than we are, we use perfumes both inward and outward to seem sweeter, wear corked shoes to seem taller, use courteous salutations to seem kinder, lowly obeisance to seem humbler, and grave and godly communication to seem wiser and devouter than we be.

17 Persian merchants in Venice. Notice the rich cloth and evidence of grandeur and wealth

There were thieves everywhere, waiting to detach the tempting hanging-pocket which everybody wore. The following story gives a vivid picture of a citizen's house and shop in the late sixteenth century:

One time, about Candlemas, when daylight shuts in about six of the clock, a cunning knave watched the house. And seeing the mistress go forth with her maid, the goodman and his folks very busy in the shop, up the stairs he goes and lifting up the latch of the hall-door, saw nobody near to trouble him. Stepping into the next chamber, where the citizen and his wife usually slept, at the bed's feet there stood a handsome trunk, wherein was very good linen, a fair gilt salt, two silver French bowls for wine, two silver drinking pots, a stone jug covered with silver and a dozen silver spoons. This trunk he brings to the stair's head and draws it down the steps so softly as he could for it was so big and heavy as he could not easily carry it. Outside the door he stood struggling with it to lift it up on the stall. The goodman coming forth of his shop to bid a customer or two farewell, made the fellow afraid he should now be caught, but calling his wits together he stood gazing up at the sign belonging to the house, as though he were desirous to know what sign it was. The Citizen came to him and asked him what he was looking for. 'I look for the sign of the Blue Bell, Sir' quoth the fellow, 'where a gentleman having taken a chamber for this term-time hath sent me with this his trunk of clothing'. Quoth the Citizen 'I know no such sign in this street, but in the next there is such a one indeed and there dwelleth one that letteth forth chambers to gentlemen'. 'Truly Sir', quoth the fellow, 'that's the house I should go to. I pray you, Sir, lend me your hand to help the trunk on my back for I can hardly get it up again'. The Citizen, not knowing his own trunk, helps him up with it and so sends him away with his own goods. When the trunk was missed, I leave to your conceits, what household grief there was on all sides.

The medieval idea had been that there was a single, just price for everything and that this price should be maintained for the good of everybody, but sixteenth-century Englishmen and their wives had to learn to think differently. Times were changing rapidly and they were faced with steep rises in the prices of all goods. This was due to a number of causes, about the relative importance of which historians still disagree: to a rising population and a consequent shortage of food; to an enormous influx of gold and silver into Europe from the New World, some of which found its way into England and lowered the purchasing power of the coinage; to heavy government expenditure in the wars with Spain; to the rage for foreign goods, wealthy ladies in particular despising anything that was not 'far-fetcht[1] and dear-bought'; and to a great expansion of trade of all kinds.

The cloth trade was still England's main support, her 'staple', as wool had been for centuries before. But now merchants were looking further afield. Bristol ships sailed to the Newfoundland fishing banks, and east coast fishermen fought with Scots, Germans, and Norwegians off the Icelandic coast. To increase consumption of fish the Queen ordered that Wednesday should be a day of abstinence from meat as well as Friday.

The explorations of sailors such as Hawkins, Frobisher, and Chancellor were followed by organized commerce and the

[1] Far-fetcht meaning, literally, brought from afar. Fashion demanded goods with the stamp of Italy or Spain or Flanders on them

Crown subsidized many trading companies. The Levant Company imported wines, olives, and currants from the Near East, the Barbary Company traded with Morocco, the Russia Company with Moscow, and the Eastland Company shipped dyed and finished cloth to Scandinavia and brought back tar and hemp and other stores.

There was a widespread conviction in England that the export of raw materials gave work and opportunity to foreign craftsmen and produced in return a flow of useless fripperies. Early in the century there were riots against foreign workmen, but later the authorities encouraged them to come, in the belief that this would develop home industries. But many English people complained that these foreigners were undermining well-established local crafts like those of the cap-makers of Chester, the lace-makers of Bristol, and the thread-makers of Coventry.

It was frequently recommended that home manufacture would benefit if duties were imposed on foreign goods. A pamphlet of 1549 urged a duty of 4s or 5s on many goods:

> There is noo waye more certene to cause all kinde of wares to be wrought within this Realme, which heretofore were wonte to be brought frome other countryes . . . it is welnighe incredible howe greate commoditie shall thereby ensue unto all Cappers, Hatters, Poyntters, Pinners, Glasemakers, Worstede weuers, Cutlers, Pewterers, Silke-women, Glovers, pursemakers and unto all occupacions and artificers which worke eney wares whereof the lyke kinde commith frome beyonde the Sees.

The anonymous writer of the pamphlet had another bee in his bonnet, too, for he adds:

> And then shall this only Subsidie do more goode to moderate the excesse of apparrell than ever eney statute have donne or cane doe in that behalfe.

The growing inflation was sufficient to worry everybody, particularly the poor, though every section of society blamed the others for the situation. One north countryman was so alarmed that he carved on the front of his house:

> this house was builded in the fourth year of the reign of King Edward the sixth, when a bushel of wheat was at 7s, a bushel of beer a noble [5s 8d], malt at 3s and more.

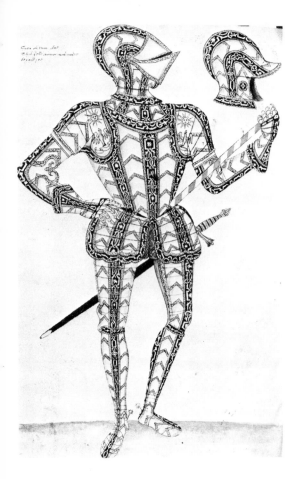

18   This exquisitely worked suit of armour is an example of fine craftmanship from the Greenwich Armoury, about 1580

A great deal of Tudor legislation showed a real concern for social justice and frequent price regulation was meant to keep essential foods within the means of the poorest section of the community. Corn, wine, and other victuals were regulated from time to time, as were also wood, wool, and bowstaves, an important item to the many who still practised archery regularly. In addition, the export of corn and fish was limited or forbidden in times of shortage; in 1597, for example, the Privy Council restricted the quantities of herring that could be exported from Yarmouth.

Prices and the conditions under which a particular trade could be carried on had for long been locally controlled, but during the sixteenth century municipal control was gradually replaced by state control. Civil war was still the chief fear in the minds of all English men and women and the need for strong centralized government was widely accepted, even by those whom it did not favour. Justices of the Peace could grant the right to set up trade and the influence of the Crown in these matters was considerable. Housewives in Cornwall would surely have been relieved to know of orders such as these, 'for the reformation of the unreasonable prices of victuals in markets in 1550':

> That the said justices within their circuits and limits to them appointed, do treat with the best and most honest personages of any market-towns . . . then to know of them what the names of those were that have sold at excessive prices, sithence [since] the late commandment . . .
>
> . . . that henceforth no fisher make sale of any kind of fish upon the sea, nor elsewhere but upon the strand; and that the same remain upon the strand during one whole hour, to be sold to al comers of the country, at such prices as one of the said fishers and one of the landmen shall appoint. And in case none of the country be there to buy the said fish, by the space of one hour that then the said fishers shall be at liberty to sel the same . . . to their most advantage, as they and the buyers may agree.

Although Guild influence was declining, we still come across reports of fines being imposed on faulty workmen, in the interests of the domestic consumer. There is an instance of this in the Records of the City of Norwich in 1524:

> John Howse, tailor, is accused by the wardens of the taylor's craft for that he would not suffer the said wardens to search in his shop in matters concerning the occupation of tailor's craft. And also for default of workmanship of a kirtle and a petticoat found by the wardens, and other misdemeanors. Whereupon he is fined 16d and to give the guild a pound candle of wax.

And, again in Norwich, in 1564, the 'Clarke of the Markett' found on March 4th:

> . . . that John Faberclyff, miller, doth kepe pullery as hennes, duckes, pygges, and swyne contrary to ther charge . . . that the gyplers, viz Alys Broune, Margery Dinglow, Thomas Moyes, and twenty others, do sell they ale and beare with pottes unsyzed and sealyd and also they do not sell a quart of the best ale or neare for a halfpenny . . . that the Cittie hathe neyther common beams, ballsunces nor waightes . . .

43

Sturbridge Fair near Cambridge was an important trading centre for centuries, and people flocked there. In 1601 the Queen had to intervene in an unusual disagreement between the University and the town about the 'King's Beam' used for weighing articles sold at the fair. Each party to the dispute claimed the exclusive right to use the Beam. Queen Elizabeth wrote:

To our loving friends the Vice chancellor and Proctors of the University of Cambridge and the Mayor and Burgesses of the Town: whereas there were at the last Sturbridge Fair some contentions about a pair of scales used by you of the University; We require you of the Town in all peaceable sort to suffer the University to exercise and use the same in the accustomed place as they have usually done . . . and what contention soever shall seem to arise about the same scales, either for the interest of the ground whereon they are settled, or for the payment of any rent for the same, We think it fit and so we require of you, that it be peacefully reconciled hereafter in a lawful course, without giving any occasion of disorders. And so We heartily bid you farewell. Aug 27, 1601

It is virtually impossible to get an accurate idea of the average income of the Elizabethan working man. The value of money was entirely different, people's needs were simpler, and they knew nothing of many things which we think are essential. But it is interesting to read of the expenses of a baker at the end

19 Two details from *The Allegory of Commerce* by Jost Amman

of the century, in an account produced as evidence that the baker was running his business at a loss:

Weekly expenses:	£	s	d
House rent at £30 per annum		11	6
Diet of man and wife 10/–; of 3 children 7/–		17	0
Diet of 4 journeymen, 2 apprentices, 2 maids	1	12	0

Clothing of man, wive and apprentice @ £20 pa	7	8
Clothing and schooling of 3 children	3	0
Wages of 4 journeymen @ 2/6; or 2 maids @ 10d	11	8
Yeast 10/–, wood 12/–, coal 1/4, sacks 1/–, salt 1/–, boulters 1/–, garner rent 2/–, baskets 3d, water 8d	1 9	3
Miller's toll 15/–, porters' fees 2/-	17	0
Parson, Poor rate, scavenger, Watch	1	0

Total expense of baking 6 quarters of wheat into bread	£6 10s 1d	

Countrywomen were able to keep their homes relatively warm with wood gathered locally and, in many districts, with charcoal. In London, however, poor families suffered a great deal, owing to the increase in the price of 'sea cole' – so called because it came south by boat from open-cast pits in Northumberland and Durham. In 1595 the Privy Council wrote to the Bishop of Durham:

> The prices of sea coles are of late risen to very high rates within the city of London, to the great oppression of the poorer sorts of people, who do use the same for their chiefest fuel . . .

Timber was becoming scarce, too, for so much of it had been used recklessly for centuries, for houses, furniture, wagons, and ships as well as fuel.

Although trade was expanding fast, it was not easy for an ambitious merchant, or anybody else, to find capital, and it was hard for the authorities to enforce legal limits to loans or interest. The uncertainties of foreign trade, or the wish to expand stock held in a family shop, could throw even careful men into the clutches of the 'usurer'. Moneylenders were very powerful, and Shakespeare wrote *The Merchant of Venice* for the entertainment of a public already sadly familiar with Antonio's kind of predicament.

Sixteenth-century English merchants were in many ways less efficient than their European counterparts. The confusion in weights and measures which had so complicated medieval trading was now much less, but accounting was far from clear in even the best of businesses. Double-entry book-keeping had been known in Italy for two centuries, but most Tudor merchants seem to have managed with a single-entry system. Text books on double-entry accounting were published in England from 1543 onwards, and one writer complained that many merchants' ledgers were

> so grossly, obscurely and lewedly kept, that after their decease neither wife, servant, executor, nor other could by their books perceive what of right appertaineth to them to be received of other, neither what justly was due by them unto other.

Many merchants were beginning to change their line of business. From being buyers and sellers of all things to all men who could afford to buy, the more far-seeing among them began to deal in larger quantities of a narrower range of goods. It was no longer as usual as it had been for a craftsman, the maker of goods, to sell them on his own premises. More and more men who had in earlier times been makers – cobblers, saddlers, and the like – were now simply retail traders who had never made anything themselves. These middlemen were reviled and blamed for being parasites, degrading the craftsmen and exploiting the customers, but their efforts undoubtedly contributed greatly to the steadily rising standards of comfort and convenience.

Food traders were not allowed the new commercial freedom that was permitted to others. Civic authorities were conservative in their approach to food prices and were fearful that the growing population and overcrowding in the towns might cause widespread suffering if ever food supplies should fail.

But the authorities were fighting a losing battle; foodstuffs were increasingly being sold in inns and taverns in London, and in nearby small towns a new class of wholesale food dealers became rich by providing goods for London tradesmen. London fruiterers, butchers, poulterers, and fishmongers no longer waited in the City for supplies to be brought to them by producers. They now ignored the medieval law about 'forestalling' and began to buy direct from producers in the countryside. The forces of economic growth were too strong; retail food shops and the wholesale organizations to supply them grew up in cities and towns everywhere, in spite of official policy.

In 1593, because of an outbreak of the plague, Queen Elizabeth issued a proclamation that Bartholomew Fair should not be held, as usual, in Smithfield. Only horses and cattle could be sold there, and 'stall wares', such as butter and cheese

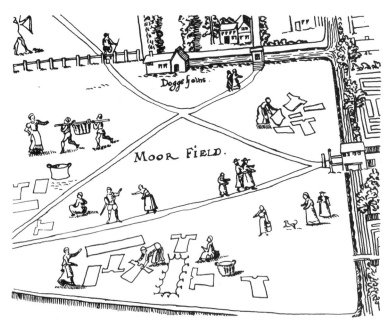

20 Detail from a map of Moorfields, London, dated 1559, showing laundresses at work

could only be sold in gross and not by retail. Woollen and linen cloths, also to be sold only in gross, were to be taken within St Bartholomew's churchyard where shops were allowed to remain open. To our, much later, knowledge of infection and contagion, it would seem that the open ground at Smithfield would have been less dangerous than an enclosed area.

House prices and rents do not perhaps come strictly into a consideration of shopping habits, but they have at all times been the first call upon the budget of most families and therefore have considerably influenced the amount of cash available for more day-to-day shopping. Poor peasants inevitably suffered most from the inflation in the sixteenth century, but many landlords were in difficulties too and found the rents they received quite inadequate because of rising prices. The situation has a strangely modern ring to it.

Some land was held by copyholders whose annual rents had been fixed more than a century before and could not legally be raised; some was held by tenants owning long leases at rents

48

which could only be raised occasionally. But some landlords then, as now, found ways round the law by putting up the premium which a tenant's heir had to pay to the landlord before he could inherit the tenancy. There was an outcry in some regions against 'rack-renting', the imposition of an excessive or extortionate rent. The term is interesting – referring to a medieval instrument of torture consisting of a frame on which a victim was fastened to rollers by wrists and ankles and had the joints of his limbs stretched by their rotation.

A man living in Pembrokeshire at the end of the century wrote of the misfortunes of the leaseholder in his area, which was notoriously poor:

> . . . now the poor tenant that lived well in that golden world is taught to sing unto his lord a new song . . . He standeth so in bodily fear of his greedy neighbour that two or three years ere his lease end, he must bow to his lord for a new lease, and must pinch it out many years before to heap money together.

For many families and communities living already at subsistence level such a disturbance in their livelihood was disastrous; hundreds of villages were deserted and old maps and aerial photographs show us many places where villages stood in medieval times but were gone by the middle of the sixteenth century. However, the law courts were not entirely on the side of the ruling class; peasants 'complained without number' to the Tudor courts. Sometimes they got redress and greater hardships were prevented, but times were hard for many Englishmen and their families.

4 The Seventeenth Century

THE FIRST permanent English settlements in North America were made early in the seventeenth century. The merchants and others who financed many of the expeditions had the ideal of an English overseas empire which would supply the mother country with needed raw materials and would become an important market for the sale of English manufactured goods.

The discovery of the New World brought wealth and increased power to many merchants and to the noblemen who were sent to administer the new colonies. But for many years life continued to be unbearably hard for the men, women, and children living in the Indians' wilderness. They had to be entirely self-sufficing in an alien environment and only grinding hard work enabled them to overcome the physical obstacles of the new lands – the forests and swamps, the diseases, the shortage of necessities. A sense of isolation must often have driven them to near despair, and only an occasional shipload of supplies or of marriageable women saved New England from complete collapse in its pioneer days.

Francis Bacon, in his essay Of Plantations, wrote of the success of the pioneers in Virginia after 1607 and advised about the kinds of people who would make the best colonists:

> The people wherewith you plant ought to be gardeners, ploughmen, labourers, smiths, carpenters, joiners, fishermen, fowlers, with some few apothecaries, cooks and bakers.

And he advised also about provisioning:

> First look about what kind of victual the country yields of itself . . . Then consider what victual or esculent things there are which grow speedily and within the year . . . Above all, there ought to be brought store of biscuit, oatmeal, flour, meal, and the like in the beginning till bread may be had.

We can imagine the amount of making, mending, buying, and collecting of things which would precede the departure of an intending settler. There would be discussions and consultations, and contrary advice must often have been given. So any news 'from the horse's mouth' would be particularly welcome; the following is part of a letter from Edward Winslow who had recently arrived in New England. After giving optimistic news of the planting undertaken and of the relations with the Indians, he wrote 'certain useful directions for such as intend a voyage into these parts':

... Now because I expect your coming unto us with other of our friends, whose company we much desire, I thought good to advertise you of a few things needfull; be carefull to have a very good bread-roome to put your Biskets in, let your Cask for Beere and Water be Ironbound for the first tyre if not more; let not your meat be drie salted, none can better doe it than the Saylers; let your meale be so hard trodd in your Cask that you shall need an Ads or Hatchet to work it out with. Trust not too much on us for Corne at this time ... be carefull to come by some of your meale to spend by the way . . . bring good store of clothes, and bedding with you; bring every man a Musket or fowling Peece . . . bring juyce of Lemons, and take it fasting, it is of good use; for hot waters, Anni-seed water is the best, but use it sparingly; bring . . . Butter or Sallet oyle . . . bring Paper, and linced oyle for your Windowes, with Cotton yarne for your Lamps . . . bring store of Powder and shot . . . so I take my leave, commending you to the LORD for a safe conduct unto us. Resting in him Plimmouth in New-England

this 11 of December

1621   Your loving Friend
                                                      E.W.

And the Reverend Francis Higginson, the first Minister at Salem wrote: 'Before you come be careful to be strongly instructed what things to bring with you for your more comfortable passage at sea and also for your husbandry occasions when you come to the land. For when you are once parted with England you shall meete neither markets nor fayres to buy what you want.'

It was not long before the more enterprising merchants in England were setting out to sell necessaries direct to the Settlers in their new homes. Here is a description of a trading venture from Bristol, in 1625:

Certain of the Chief Merchants of the City of Bristol . . . prepared a small ship called the Speedwell, of about 50 tons, manned with thirty men and boys, and a bark called the Discoverer of 26 tons, with thirteen men and a boy, victualled for eight months, and furnished with certain merchandise to trade with the people of the country: as hats of divers colours, apparel of coarse kersey and canvas ready-made, stockings, shoes, saws, pickaxes, hooks, knives, scissors, bells, beads, looking-glasses, thimbles, needles, thread and such like. They set sail from Milford Haven on the 10th April.

It is surprising to know at how early a date it was possible to buy English manufactured products regularly in the shops in New England. There are records that one, George Corwin, set up shop in Salem in 1651, for the sale of fabrics and hardware. His shop was well stocked and he was selling such luxuries as children's toys at a time when life in the new colonies was still very insecure. It is perhaps an indication of the dangers surrounding the early colonists, that Corwin sold a considerable variety of locks – stock locks, spring locks with screws, single and double chest locks, warded outside chest locks, outside box locks, plain cupboard locks, and small and large padlocks. A few years later this small shop was supplying Salem inhabitants with combs, white haft knives, barbers' scissors, flour boxes, carving tools, carpenters' tools, door latches, curry combs and brushes for horses, many kinds of earthenware and woodware, needles, pins, thread, buttons, ribbons, laces, and a great variety of fabrics.

In the Public Record Office, in London, there are returns of outward and inward entries at the colonial ports, which testify to a flourishing trade, most of which would be to the advantage of English merchants selling in Bristol, Plymouth, and Liverpool.

The invoice of an importation into Boston at the end of the century contained such items as brass curtain rings, dressing glasses, square monument candlesticks, brass extinguishers, tin lanterns, pocket nutmeg graters, bread graters, wooden rat traps with springs, carved spoons, beer taps, hair sieves, sucking bottles, and milk trays.

The early settlers in America had little coinage for circulation and had to barter materials and goods. Pelts were very much valued and the Indians were ready to barter them for beads, knives, hatchets, powder, shot guns, and 'strong water'. In most of the colonies Indian wampum[1] was extensively used and often paid into the treasury in payment of taxes. So also were corn, cattle, and musket balls. In Virginia tobacco was used for

[1] Wampum was small beads made from mollusc shells. Even Harvard College tuition fees were paid in wampum at one time

21 Tavern scene from the Roxburgh Ballads. Notice the
long table which customers normally shared.

currency and 'from 100 to 150 pounds of it bought many a man
a good wife'.

In New England, beer was the first luxury to be imported,
but soon the Puritan colonists learned to use Indian corn and
other ingredients. Among the jottings in the seventeenth-
century diary of James Samuel Sewell of New England there
are surprising references to the import of such varied beverages
as ale, beer, canary, brandy, chocolate, cider, claret, mead,
metheglin, punch, sack, sage-tea, sillabub, and wine. Various
strong white wines imported from Southern Europe were
classified as 'sack' and Governor Winthrop, in his writings in
1646, mentioned the arrival in port of 800 butts of sack on board
four ships.

Metheglin and mead, though mild and made from honey,
yeast, and water, were very intoxicating. Governor Bradford, in

22 A French bakery. Notice the bread oven in the background

discussing two hogsheads of metheglin which were to be delivered from England, reported that six gallons actually arrived, because merry-makers on board the ship *Friendshippe* decided to 'drink it up under the name leakage'!

In spite of King James' denunciation of smoking and his gloomy forebodings about the future of 'a province built on smoake', Virginia soon began to specialize in the cultivation of tobacco. In exchange, Bristol merchants sent household goods of every kind, plantation implements, clothing for slaves, and luxuries for the planters, but, most of all, indentured labourers. Tobacco served as currency in the southern colonies and it is recorded that in 1698, in Thirdhaven, Maryland, 'John Stacey having covered and ceiled our great meeting-house, there is due unto him 2,000 pounds of tobacco'.

There was relatively little money available in the colonies and there were no banks in which to deposit savings. So it was important for anyone wishing to accumulate capital to buy land and to collect some of the basic domestic articles, even though they might not be needed for use. This was especially true of objects which had to be imported from overseas; clothes and household furnishings represented money in the bank, so many wealthy settlers accumulated them in very large quantities.

This was a prosperous time in England, the shortages and inefficiencies of earlier times were being overcome and much of the new wealth was spent in what we call 'consumer durables'. Shop-*keeping* gradually became freed from the rules and constraints which had been accepted for so long; there was more wealth about and wealthy customers to be wooed.

More and more men were finding retail trade a dignified way of life and were establishing for themselves a profitable and respectable position midway between the makers of goods and the buyers of them. They began to supply materials to workmen to make up at home, and they bought back the finished products and sold them. This happened in many trades, such as book-selling, for example. Whereas Caxton and his successors had taken orders for books direct from the public and had sold them at their workshops, now book*selling* gradually became an important trade in its own right, quite apart from book printing or book binding.

Inevitably craftsmen who made such individual things as spectacles, musical instruments, tobacco pipes, firearms, clocks, and watches continued to sell them direct to the customer, who usually needed to discuss his personal requirements with the expert on his own premises. But it could no longer be assumed that a saddler *made* saddles, or a glover, gloves; each could equally well be a retail shopkeeper, buying-in a variety of items from a number of different makers. Though it was a further three centuries before a baker was normally a seller, rather than a maker of bread.

All these changes brought great novelty and variety to London shops; provincials were attracted to the capital and London became the shop-window for the whole country.

But there was no standard 'shop' and the word was often used to describe any place where anything was sold. An 'open' shop had little more than a roof supported by poles, with a board below; a 'standing' shop seems often to have been the front room of a house; and by the end of the century the word had come to mean most of the ground floor selling area in front with storage, and probably accounting, behind. By then, many shops had their windows glazed with small leaded panes, with wooden shutters which were taken down in the morning and put up at closing time. There is reference in *The London Spy*, a book published in 1698, to 'the joyful alarm of Bow Bell which called the weary apprentices from their work to unhitch their folded shutters and button up their shops till the next morning'.

There was strict control by city authorities of the size of the boards and shutters of street shops. In London no board could project more than 2½ feet into the street, and if the upper part of the shutters was swung up on hinges to protect the board from rain or sun, posts and signboards had also to be of this minimum height.

Most customers were still inveigled into a purchase by the shopkeeper, or his apprentice, standing outside their shop and shouting 'What lack ye? What lack ye?'. But some of the more up-to-date shops had begun to display their goods attractively in the hope of attracting the eyes of passers by. This trivial practice was frowned upon by many puritans who disapproved of such encouragement to extravagance. But a French writer, in 1663, was full of praise for London shopping:

> There is no City in the World that has so many and such fine shops. For they are large and their decorations are as valuable as those of the stage. The scene is now everywhere which exceedingly pleases and attracts the eye as we go along.

The smartest shops in seventeenth-century London were in Cheapside and on London Bridge. In Elizabeth's reign Cheapside had been monopolized by goldsmiths and silk mercers but by the time of Charles I milliners, booksellers, stationers, drugsters, linen drapers, and others were thriving there. The merchants of Cheapside still found it advantageous to allow their wives to sit outside their shops, to chat to passers by and entice them in. The wit and beauty of these Cheapside women was well known. In Shakespeare's *As You Like It* Jacques says 'You are full of pretty answers. Have you not been acquainted with goldsmiths' wives and conned them out of rings?'.

London Bridge was still the only bridge over the Thames, and was still lined on both sides with tall houses, so to the shoppers it must have seemed like any other crowded London street. In

23 *The Gallerie du Palais.* Obviously fashionable, this book-shop was for the wealthy to while away their spare time

1633 a bad fire destroyed forty-one of the shops on London Bridge and it is interesting that nearly all of them were connected with clothing. There were eight 'Haberdashers of Small Wares', three 'Haberdashers of Hattes', six Hosiers, two Mercers, two Glovers, a Girdler, a Silkman, and others. Trade was brisk, for there was a constant stream of people walking over to Bankside to enjoy the bearbaiting and the theatres which were banned from the City.

As fashions became more and more elaborate, second-hand clothes sellers did a brisk business. These shopkeepers called themselves 'brokers' because they also lent money on clothes, but their main business was to buy and sell whatever clothes were brought to them and, according to Stubbes, a great many of these were stolen goods. It seems that one very successful trick was to catch garments with hook and line through an open window as their owners were asleep! Stubbes, in *The Anatomie of Abuses*, referred to 'this dung-hill trade of brokery, newly sprung up' but the practice was legal and regulations were

24 Dutch silk spinners and apprentices working
at home, 1695

made concerning it. An Order in Council of 1670 stated that
brokers must not 'make any outward shew, or hang forth on
their Stalls, Shop-boards or Windows towards any Street, any
of the Apparel to be sold'.

London was, of course, in no way typical of shopping habits
and opportunities. Most people still lived in the country and
were obliged to be largely self-sufficient. Adaptability and
inventiveness were first necessities in running a household,
however large or small. Seasonal variations, changes in trading
customs, royal decisions regarding monopolies, rights, and
coinage – all these factors could upset established patterns of
provisioning for the rich as much as for the poor.

But London continued to be the source for many items of

special interest to well-to-do families. Imported luxuries such as tobacco, table glasses, wax torches, Rhenish wine, Westphalian ham, and neates' tongues were listed by the household treasurer of the Earl of Rutland at Belvoir Castle. Spices from India, currants from Greece, timber from the Baltic countries, silks from Asia, porcelain and lacquered furniture from the Orient, ivory and slaves from Africa – all these found ready buyers in London.

During the first half of the seventeenth century the rise in prices was among the most important of social changes. The population was increasing, rising expectations helped to force up the cost of necessities, and several bad harvests between 1630 and 1637 made things worse. Many shop-keepers must have had difficulty in making any sort of a living from their selling and most probably did other work on the side, like Roger Lowe of Leigh in Lancashire who often obliged his neighbours by writing letters for them, and making out wills for sick people.

One of the difficulties of a small shop-keeper at this time was that of unpaid bills. Currency was still scarce and because of this it was not uncommon for quite well-to-do people to take a long time to pay their debts. A Quaker shop-keeper wrote, in 1687: 'It being now a year since I began trade, I find I have been too forward in trusting, too backward in calling, as is frequent with young tradesmen.'

Women were considered to be specially qualified for shop-keeping or any sort of trading and in *The Household Account Book* of Sarah Fell of Swarthmoor Hall, Lancashire, there are frequent references to buying from 'Goodwife' so-and-so. The Fells were a prominent Quaker family, closely related to George Fox, and in the minute books of Monthly Meetings there are frequent references to sums paid to provide poor widows with stock with which to set up shop. For example, in March 1689 Friends were directed to 'visitt ye widow Smith . . . and if they see ocatione to hand something to her as a stock . . . a little trade not exceeding 20s' and in October 1696 it is entered 'paid Mary Fairman for ye widdow Thomas as a stock for hur to buy something to sell againe 10s'.

The immigration of Huguenot refugees from France after 1648 was an enormous stimulus to trade in England and helped to raise the standard of living. Silk weavers settled in Spitalfields and fashionable men and women were delighted to buy their

59

new silk velvets and damasks for elegant gowns, waistcoats and cloaks, as well as for wall hanging and upholstery covering. Linen factories were set up in Ipswich and in Scotland, where an Act for burying corpses in Scots linen was passed, in order to encourage the growth of flax. The hat trade also benefited greatly from the immigrants, for French trappers had for over a century caught beaver in Canada and had developed ways of preparing the skins and sticking them to hats. Paper-making, watch-making, and clock-making were other arts owed to foreigners. These and other new economic ventures led to a growth in size and importance of such towns as Birmingham, Sheffield, Manchester, and Bristol. The population of Birmingham, for example, increased sevenfold between 1685 and 1725. Men already began to say of England then what in fact was not fully true till the 1870s, that half the people lived in towns.

There was new and increasing confidence in both wholesale and retail trade. People were beginning to realize that in a vigorous and growing community competition could work better than state regulation. Medieval systems of control, like the assizes of bread, of beer, of cloth, and the Guild regulations, had been suited to a country with little capital to invest, where

25 Silversmiths at work, late seventeenth century. The men on the right are beating the metal into shape

the internal communications were very poor and where people were uneducated and unadventurous. Now, change and expectancy were in the air and ambitions were no longer confined to the very rich.

The development of English commerce was greatly helped, too, by Jewish immigration. During nearly four centuries, between the expulsion of the Jews by Edward I in 1290 to their re-admission under Cromwell, few Jews had taken any prominent part in commerce or trade. There was a large Jewish settlement in Holland – where Rembrandt painted many of them so lovingly – and there the Jews carried on exchange and banking transactions very successfully. Many English merchants were envious of the low rate of interest at which their Dutch rivals could borrow capital, and welcomed the permission given by Cromwell for Jews to live and trade in England.

Increased trade and more work meant that people were able to save money and, for some time, there had been concern as to where it should best be kept for safety. Thomas Dekker, in *The Seven deadly Sins of London* written in 1606, refers to money as a commodity like any other:

> . . . hammers are beating in one place, tubs hooping in another, pots clinking in a third, water tankards running at tilt in a fourth. Here are porters sweating under burdens, there merchants' men bearing bags of money.

and another writer refers to a scarcity of money which 'proceeds from the late practice of bringing up the Tax-Money in Wagons to London' – presumably a good deal was stolen by highwaymen on the way.

Gradually the goldsmiths of London, whose normal work was, of course, to make and sell gold and silver vessels, began to look after people's money for them. Their business compelled them to take special precautions against theft and most people seem to have had confidence in their honesty.

In Italy there had been deposit banks since the fifteenth century. In the seventeenth century banks were established in Amsterdam, in Hamburg, and in Sweden, but in England there was no public bank until after the Civil War. The Bank of England was established in the 1690s.

Counterfeit coinage was being produced in such serious

quantities that in 1662 new coinage had to be minted. *The Kingdom's Intelligencer* for 22 August of that year contained the following notice:

> Whitehall. Aug. 22. There hath been a discovery of divers persons who have coined both gold and silver, and of other persons who have vended the same in great quantities, intending to utter the same to clothiers and at Fairs; which is published to an end that honest persons may not be deceived by receiving such monies.

The redoubtable Celia Fiennes travelled all over the country and left fascinating descriptions of the many houses she visited. Of shops she has little to say, but she found that in Newcastle, in 1699: 'Their shops are good and of distinct trades, not selling many things in one shop as is the custom in most country towns and cities . . .' Not everybody at the time thought that the great increase in shop-keeping throughout the country was to the general advantage. In 1684 one writer complained:

> For now in every country village . . . there is a shopkeeper, and one that never served any apprenticeship to any shopkeeping trade whatsoever. And many of these are not such that do deal only in pins and such small wares, but . . . in as many substantial commodities as any that live in cities and market towns and who have no less than a thousand pounds worth of goods in their shops, for which they pay not one farthing of any tax at all, either parochial or national . . .

These country shops did not sell food, for they had no storage suitable for perishable goods; and at this time, and for another two centuries at least, a large proportion of the food for an ordinary family was provided entirely by the women and children belonging to it. Until the eighteenth century food buying was 'marketing' and not 'shopping'.

Fortunately there are a number of Household Account Books which have survived and can tell us a good deal about the provisioning of a grand country household of the time. The Clerk of the Kitchen at Woburn Abbey kept a 'Kitchen-Book' which was signed by the Duke of Bedford himself every week. Here were recorded all expenses for food for the household and for visitors; there was also a petty cash book in which were recorded such items as mops, brushes, cleaning materials, and many yards of coarse cloth used for making bags and dusters. The Clerk needed, too, a small amount of cash in hand to

26 Interior of a shop 1685. Notice the rich garments of the nobleman

reward the messengers who brought goods to the house, and also to pay the pedlars who supplied such articles as thread, needles, and tape, for the use of the sewing maids. All these details had to be approved by the Earl's signature.

Beer was made at home by rich and poor, but we read of a large household in Leicestershire importing French claret, Rhenish wines, sherry, and canary in hogsheads (63 gallons) and puncheons (84 gallons).

Coffee gradually became known in England after the middle of the century and by 1690 it was available in comparatively large quantities. From 1670 the Earl of Bedford's accounts at Woburn Abbey record the occasional purchase of very small quantities of coffee for the personal use of himself and the Countess. In 1670, too, there is mention of the purchase of a coffee pot, a china dish, and 9s worth of coffee. From 1685 one pound of coffee powder appears as a regular item in the grocery

27 Shops on the ice at the Frost Fair, London 1683–4

bill, for the general use of the household. Chocolate was less popular at first, but was drunk increasingly during the next century, and tea gained favour steadily.

There seems to have been little system in the provisioning of even large households and this was probably inevitable at a time when supplies were determined by random matters like the weather, a chance meeting of seller and buyer, or the frequently changing fiscal policy of king or parliament. The markets were still the source of much that was needed. 'Bay-salte' – top quality from the Bay of Biscay – could be bought at Stourbridge; 'Mattes for to lay under feather bedds, being rough and shaggie' at Loughborough; woven rush matting, a new luxury, was ordered from Norfolk by up-to-date households all over the country. The Household Book for Naworth Castle, on the Scottish border, records a constant coming and going in order to keep family and retainers supplied with necessaries: saddles and other riding equipment from Hexham, boots and shoes from Penrith, candles from Kendal, linen from both Yorkshire and Lancashire, small items from pedlars at the gate of the castle. But most things were made at home.

At this time scarcely any roads existed in England, except round London, Norwich, York, Bristol, and a few other towns. Wheel traffic was probably unknown in the Swarthmoor district, for example, and all Sarah Fell's purchases must have been carried on pack saddles: wine and 'Hollands cheese' from Newcastle, oranges and gloves from London through Kendal, a basket from Bristol, a box from York (how one would like to know what they were for!), and various things from Worcester. Swarthmoor Hall required more than usual foresight on the housekeeper's part, since Lancaster, the nearest shopping town, was some 20 miles distant by road across two estuaries passable for only a few hours each day.

In more modest households, with fewer servants to occupy and fewer resources of land or influence to draw upon, more goods were of necessity bought in. The Reverend Giles Moore, a vicar in Kent, bought many items ready made, and recorded:

7 May 1656. I bought of Mr Clowson, upholster itinerant living over against the crosse at Chichester but who comes about the country with his packs on horseback.

A large fine coverlett with birds and bucks	£2	10s	
A sett of striped curtaines and valance	£1	8s	
A coarse coverlett	£1	2s	
2 middle blankettes	£1	13s	6d
One Holland tyke or bolster	£1	4s	

Bread was the basic food for everybody. In the country it was home-made, but in the towns it was on sale from bakers' wives or apprentices standing with their baskets and crying 'Hot Bread! Hot Bread!'

Many bakers specialized in coarse brown bread for poorer customers and in horse-bread. Every loaf had to be stamped either with an 'H' for brown, or 'housewives' bread, or a 'W' for wheaten, or white bread. It also had to be marked with the baker's seal which was registered at the Hall of the Bakers' Company, so that any loaf which was unsatisfactory could be traced to its source. Bakers baked dough brought to them by those who had no oven of their own, and taverns and cookshops often sold their surplus loaves illegally at the back door, so that the standards of quality set by the Bakers' Company were difficult to maintain.

Meat was the next most valued food, but the poor rarely tasted any except offal, tripe, or trotters. From contemporary accounts we get an impression of a constant shortage of beef everywhere. When it was bought in towns it must have been tough and stringy, since all animals were reared on an indifferent diet and their muscles would be toughened on the long trek from the countryside. Butchers were considered a deceitful race and, indeed, their tricks were very varied. We read of fat being pinned onto joints to improve their appearance and of butchers who, against normal usage, left all the blood in their meat to add to the weight.

Scales were still very expensive items, kept by only very few traders, and housewives were accustomed to buying everything by appearance. According to the Butchers' Company's regulations in 1607, lamb must not be cut 'deceitfully' but must have ten ribs in the forequarter and three in the hindquarter, and no piece cut off in between could be sold. And as late as 1667, a pamphlet entitled *What England Wants* urged that most food exposed for sale in markets and shops should be sold by weight 'as is done in Spain'.

Quantities bought were much bigger than they normally are nowadays, which seems surprising since it must have been difficult to keep foodstuffs fresh. There is never mention of buying less than 'a fish'; and 'a cheese'; butter, heavily salted, was sold in barrels; Stow refers to the price of 'one hundredweight of beef' and when, in February 1601, the Steward to the Earl of Rutland went shopping for food, he bought, among a great quantity of other things, 'half a lamb' and 'two heron'.

Fish was eaten a great deal in London and the fishwives, those 'disorderly lewd women and maids fitted for painful and laborious service', were an old London institution. A description of them in 1632 states that:

These crying, wandering and travelling creatures carry their shops on their heads and their storehouse is ordinarily Billingsgate or the Bridge-foot. They set up every morning their trade afresh. They are easily set up and furnished, get something and spend it jovially and merrily. Five shillings, a basket and a good cry, is a large stock for one of them . . . They are free of all places and pay no shop-rent, but only find repairs to it. If they drink out their whole stock, its but pawning a petticoat in Long Lane or themselves in Turnbull Street for to set up again. When they have done their fair they meet in mirth, singing and dancing and, in the middle, scolding. When in any evening they are not merry in a drinking-house it is suspected they have had bad return or else have paid some old score or else are bankrupts.

Medicinal herbs too were regularly hawked about the streets as we read in one of the Roxburgh ballads:

> Here's pennyroyal and marygolds,
> Come, buy my nettle tops!
> Here's water-cress and scurvy-grass,
> Come buy my sage of virtue ho!
> Come, buy my wormwood and mugworts,
> Here's all fine herbs of every sort!
> Here's southern-wood that's very good,
> Dandelion and housekeel!
> Here's dragon's tongue, and wood-sorrel,
> With bear's-foot and horehound!
> Let none despise the merry, merry cries
> Of famous London Town!

For centuries it had – rightly – been considered dangerous to drink raw milk, but by the seventeenth century there was a Milk House in St James's Park where people could drink a glass of

28 The village cobbler at work, from a painting by Jan Victors

freshly warm milk in clean and attractive surroundings. In many places cows were led from door to door, so that their milk could be drawn directly into the customers' jugs. On May morning the milkmaids called at their customers' houses for a traditional tip. On May morning 1667, Samuel Pepys wrote that he went: 'To Westminster, on the way meeting with many milk-maids with garlands upon their pails, dancing, with a fiddler before them.'

The first type of merchants to sell food in shops, as opposed to stalls in markets, were grocers. Most of the goods they sold were imported and so their business did not conflict with that of those who were selling fresh foodstuffs, but they did overlap with apothecaries who, for example, sold to the Duke of Bedford's steward, in 1653, 'skurvy grass or gittings to put in the childrens ale'.

And a few years later the Steward received this bill:

Bought of Ansell Carter, grocer, July 1658:	£	s	d
Case nutmegs, 2 lbs		13	4
½ cwt currents at 6d per lb	1	8	0
½ cwt malagas at 2½d per lb		11	8
2 cwt sugar at 6d per lb	5	12	0
cloves 1 lb		8	0
large mace		8	0
large cinnamon		3	7
large ginger, 1 lb		1	9
rice 2 lbs			8
prunes 6lbs		1	3
white candy 1 lb		2	6
jordan almonds 1 lb		1	6
2 boxes and corss [presumably to put the purchases in]		4	0

The food markets of London, according to Stow in his *Survey of London*, were 'unmeasureably pestred with the unimaginable increase and multiplicity of market-folkes'. There were at that time no less than twelve old-established retail markets, most of them in busy streets. Hundreds of trestles filled the streets and hundreds of sellers stood about with goods for sale in sack or basket, calling out their wares and jostling with passers by. Pepys, in 1666, wrote of 'driving through the backside of the Shambles in Newgate Market, when my coach plucked down two pieces of beef into the dirt upon which the butchers stopped the horses and a great rout of people in the street . . .'

The Great Fire of London which caused so much suffering at the time had many good effects in the long run. One of these was the destruction of the narrow streets in which the markets had long been held. Four new groups of buildings were erected to take all the markets off the streets. The biggest of them all – and the biggest in Europe at the time – was Leadenhall, where careful organization and control replaced the old free-for-all mixtures of goods. In one court beef was sold on 100 stalls; in another, other kinds of meat on 140 stalls. Rows of stalls selling butter were in one area, those selling fish, cheese, or fruit and vegetables in others. Leadenhall was enormous and one of the showpieces of London.

The new market buildings were all rectangular courtyards, open to the sky, because the roofing of wide areas was still a difficult and costly business. They were fine new buildings, but confusion and corruption were still rife inside. In a petition to the Lord Mayor in 1699 eight women 'being all poor people who sell small provisions in Newgate Market, viz lamb, pork, butter, eggs, oat-cakes, hoggs' puddings, sausages, etc. in small quantities, none of them ever bringing more than a horse-load into the market on any one day' complained that they were being charged 2s 6d for two days for 'moveable boards'. They held that they 'aught not to pay more than twopence a day' and referred to 'the further oppressions not complained of for fear of further extortion'. It was not until the very end of the century that the city authorities began to control the charges for stall rents and so put an end to private extortion.

5 The Eighteenth Century

By this time the English plantations in America had grown to maturity and, now that the French menace had disappeared from the St Lawrence, the colonists regarded the whole continent as potentially theirs. They were rich, energetic, and inventive, and had begun to resent strongly the supercilious attitude of the English at home and to find such terms as 'our colonies' and 'the provincials' highly objectionable. They had developed strong national feelings, but unfortunately English statesmen and merchants still continued to think of the new lands as so many kitchen gardens, existing in order to be exploited for the good of English trade.

In retaliation against increasing taxation without proper representation, the colonists used a weapon which is very much in vogue now, 200 years later. *Felix Farley's Bristol Journal* of 16 February 1765 reported ominously: '. . . many gentlemen of considerable property there [Virginia] are coming into an Agreement not to use in their Families several of the most staple Articles, the Produce of this country.' And on 16 November of the same year, a letter on the same theme from a merchant named Francis Harris, of Philadelphia, was published in the same *Journal*: 'At a general meeting of the merchants and traders of this city it was . . . resolved by them . . . that they would not import any goods from Great Britain until the Stamp Act[1] was repealed.'

But for some time longer the wealthier settlers depended upon England to provide them with fashionable goods. We know very little about how long it took for new fashions to spread westwards, but it is probable that once a new item was landed on the New England coast there was little time lag before it was available on the frontier settlements. The mid-eighteenth-century pioneer housewife who wanted, for example, a teapot would not be able to buy it from the Indians, nor would she have been likely to find a local potter with the skill to make it. She might buy it from an itinerant trader, or her husband would bring it back when he travelled to one of the coastal towns where European ships docked. The plantation gentry wrote often to agents in England, ordering – as George

[1] An imposition of stamps on all legal documents in the colonies, as a means of raising revenue.

29 A travelling 'inkman' with his barrels of ink powder

Washington did – 'silver spurs of the new'r Fashn', or asking for
chinaware or furniture of whatever styles were fashionable in
London.

Wherever there were settlers there were, of course, pedlars,
known also as packmen, hawkers, and hucksters. Each carried
his limited stock of wares in a bag or trunk on his back, or in
a cart, wagon, or boat. A vendor was a townsman who either
had a stand where he did business or else had a hand cart or
small wagon with which he toured the neighbourhood. The
icecream vendor and the hot dog vendors of today are
descendants of these men.

In time many pedlars exchanged their pack or cart for the
life of a country store-keeper. When a farmer could get to a
store only once every so often he would buy in quantity – a
barrel of flour or sugar, whisky or kerosene. And since cash was

scarce much selling was bartering or 'trading'.[2] A housewife would barter surplus preserves or quilts for salt, pepper, spices, mirrors, bibles, or whatever she happened to want at the time. In addition people who wanted services performed – an umbrella mended, a clock repaired, a tombstone cut, teeth pulled, and so on – would enquire at the store or wait until a travelling specialist came along to do such work.

30   View of the Stock Market, London 1753. Notice how some tradesmen sold their wares in the street, some from stalls

The store owner bought everything in bulk: corned beef and molasses came in hogsheads which might hold as much as 140 pounds; wine and oil came in pipes which held two hogsheads; beer and wine in butts of about the same size. Whale oil was in

[2] The word is still firmly in the American language and many a housewife of today will ask a friend 'where do you trade?'.

72

tierces, and rice too; butter in firkins, pigs' feet in kegs, lard in kilderkins, salt mackerel in tonnekins, maple syrup in piggins, lard and hams soaked in brine were sold in tubs. Other items were in boxes, crocks, pails, jute sacks, and jugs. 'Dry goods' meant most merchandise that was not weighed or poured; 'produce' meant foodstuffs that would keep and could be shipped long distances; 'groceries' were the luxuries of diet from the West Indies and southern Europe.

A merchant's chief preoccupation was obtaining the goods he needed to sell or barter. By ox cart he carried local goods – 'country pay' – to the wholesale markets in Boston, New York, or Philadelphia and exchanged them for such luxuries as English Staffordshire ware, French brandy, German glass, Holland gin, or West Indian rum. Transportation was costly and dangerous. There are records of many accidents and on one occasion a rascal cut the rope of the baggage wagon and made off with 'knives, forks, a few snuffers and trays, pocket knives, slates, Naples soap, brass lamps and candlesticks – reward ten dollars'.

After the British took over in the area of what is now New York, the stalls and open markets there were replaced by substantial buildings. One such structure, built on the shore of the East River in the 1690s, lasted over a hundred years.

In the 1730s the Oswego market was founded on Broadway, and the street was lined with long, low, rambling market buildings. Trade became very brisk and traffic so congested that, in 1771, the city authorities decided to clear Broadway of all business premises and a new market was built on the shore of the Hudson river.

According to the record 'the first meat sold in this new market was the flesh of a bear that had been killed close by as it clambered up the river bank after swimming from the Jersey shore'. From this incident the market was popularly called the Bear Market 'and was so called until the year 1814'.

Shop-keepers' newspaper advertisements tell us a lot about the taste and needs of the people of the time. The *Virginia Gazette* for 25 July 1766, for example, listed the considerable range of ceramic goods imported by a firm of Norfolk merchants:

   . . . china bowls of all sorts, plates, dishes, chocolate cups and saucers, coffee and tea cups and saucers, tea and milk pots, mugs, earthenware, chamber and spitting pots, butter tubs and stands . . . childrens' chair pans, potting pots . . . white sets of childrens toys complete . . . white, green and blue candlesticks . . . Dutch jugs . . . Dutch tiles . . . Italian lamps with floats . . . English china of all sorts.

By the beginning of the eighteenth century Bristol had already become a great port, mainly interested in colonial trade. She exported every variety of English manufacture and imported from the colonies products ranging from codfish and furs to timber, sugar, and tobacco. A great deal of Bristol capital was invested in these trades and in addition, many Bristol tradesmen were connected with the repair, equipment, lading and manning of ships. There were also numerous wood-workers, cabinet-makers, dyers, and insurance brokers whose main concern was colonial commodities.

So many goods were heavily taxed in England throughout the eighteenth century that it is not surprising that smuggling was widespread. John Pinney, merchant of Bristol, who had extensive plantations of sugar in the West Indies, was often busy helping his friends to avoid paying duties on small luxuries which they tried to smuggle into England. In his Business Letter-books of 1761–74 he wrote:

You will receive a Barrel of Sugar directed for you, and marked FH in the middle of which you will find two Potts of preserved Tamarinds, the difficulty of getting Sweetmeats landed, and conveyed Safe has induced me to take this method.

Again:

Dear Madam!

Capt Clerke being fearful that your madeira would be seized, he sent it with your chocolate, in small quantities, to my house— I sent the chocolate with your turtle last Saturday, and you will now receive 3 doz and 9 bottles of madeira wine . . .

It was largely thanks to the smugglers that tea-drinking steadily increased in England, for relatively little of it paid the customs duty of 5s a pound. Smuggling was regarded by everyone as entirely innocent, as is evident from the fact that even Parson Woodforde noted in his diary on 29 March 1777:

Andrews the smuggler brought me this night about 11 o'clock a bagg of Hyson Tea 6 pound weight. He frightened us a little by whistling under the parlour window just as we were going to bed. I gave him Geneva [gin] and paid him for the tea at 10/6d per pound.

31 West India House, Amsterdam. Holland was the centre of European trade in the seventeenth century

Tea was known by a variety of exotic-sounding names. Every customer bought and blended his own choice, mixing the cheaper Common Bohea or Common Green with Hysons, Souchongs, or Congous. Prices varied each season and the leaves were stored in little tea-caddies fitted with porcelain mixing bowls and locks to keep the contents safe from pilfering. Used tea-leaves were the perks of the cook, who made a small profit by selling them at the back door to the local poor.

The English passion for tea-drinking necessitated a ready supply of imported china cups and bowls bought from 'India' or 'China' shops which sold miscellaneous oriental wares. Tea-leaves, too, were often sold in china shops, as well as by apothecaries and in coffee houses.

There was no control over the sale of milk. When it came from farm cows it was sometimes fresh, often sour and nearly always dirty. Town cows were kept in such appallingly dirty conditions that their milk must have been the most dangerous of foods. Milkmaids carrying open cans of milk on their heads went from door to door; the open cans protected their heads from the slops and rubbish thrown from upstairs windows, but

The Paper-Mill.

Thomas Kinnersly,

BOOKSELLER, STATIONER & PUBLISHER,
At the Paper Mill,
the North Side of St. Paul's Church-Yard.

London,

Sells Books in all Languages & Faculties,
BIBLES, COMMON PRAYERS,
School Books, & all sorts of modern Books,
LIKEWISE
Letter & Pocket Book Cases of the newest
Fashion, and Stationary Wares of all Sorts
Wholesale or Retail, & great variety of Plays,
Periodical Publications of all kinds.
N.B. Ready Money for any Library
or Parcel of Books.

32   A decorative trade card

no housewife or cook can have bought milk with any confidence.

The wholesale trade was becoming more organized, employ-ing salesmen to visit shops in both town and country, and many large town shop-keepers began to develop a sideline in selling wholesale to other smaller men. This sometimes caused diffi-culties with retail customers who heard different prices quoted from those they were expected to pay. So the custom began of putting aside one part of the shop for wholesale trade, where customers came in by a back door marked 'wholesale trade only'.

Advertising was still in its infancy; some early newspapers printed 'for sale' notices but most tradesmen relied upon elegantly designed 'trade cards' that were often used as bill-heads. From the earliest times tradesmen had tried to attract customers by hanging out their signs, and as shops became more numerous and so more competitive, signs became larger and heavier and a danger to the public. There had been occasional complaints about this nuisance since medieval times but nothing was done until, in 1718, a large sign hanging in Bride Lane in London, crashed to the ground, tearing away the front of the house and killing four people. There was a public outcry against all hanging signs and in 1762 a proclamation ordered their removal. Some shop-keepers kept their sign-boards and fixed them flat to the front of the building; others put up written signboards across the doorway, with notices such as 'shoes mended here', 'children educated here', or 'foreign spirituous liquors sold here'.

'A nation of shop-keepers' the English already were in many respects, but the taunt lost much of its sting in the applause of hosts of foreign visitors to England. A Hanoverian sat upon the English throne and so German visitors felt particularly at home in London. One of the most indefatigable and most observant was Sophie de la Roche, who visited London in 1786 and wrote a diary describing in lively style her cultural and social activities. She had much to say about the streets and shops of London:

> We strolled up and down lovely Oxford Street this evening, for some goods look more attractive by artificial light. Just imagine, dear children, a street taking half an hour to cover from end to end, with double rows of brightly shining lamps, in the middle of which stands an equally long row of beautifully lacquered coaches, and on either side of these there is room for two coaches to pass one another; and the pavement inlaid with flagstones, can stand six people deep and allows one to gaze at the splendidly lit shop fronts in comfort. First one passes a watchmaker's, then a silk or fan store, now a silversmiths, a china or glass shop. Just as alluring are the confectioners and fruiterers, where, behind the

handsome glass windows, pyramids of pineapples, figs, grapes, oranges and all manner of fruits are on show.

Up to eleven o'clock at night there are as many people along this street as at Frankfurt during the fair, not to mention the eternal stream of coaches . . . the arrangement of the shops, with their adjoining living rooms, makes a very pleasant sight. For right through the excellently illuminated shop one can see many a charming family scene enacted: some are still at work, others drinking tea, a third party is entertaining a friendly visitor, in a fourth parents are joking and playing with their children.

Sophie was impressed by seeing an iron railing 'erected some few paces from [each] house' which 'runs up to the front door dividing the road from the basement' and also by the fact that, while looking at the shop windows 'people like to have their children with them and take them out in the air, and they wrap them up well, though their feet are always bare and sockless'.

Apparently it was still the custom, in London at any rate, to bleed meat before selling it for, walking in the streets near Green Park, Sophie was

interested to find the meat so fine and shops so deliciously clean; all the goods were spread on snow-white cloths and cloths of similar whiteness were stretched out behind the large hunks of meat hanging up; no blood anywhere, no dirt; the shop-walls and doors were all spruce, balance and weights brightly polished . . . Bread likewise laid out on white cloths . . .

and she was surprised to see that, in linen shops

. . . there is a cunning device for showing women's materials. They hang down in folds behind the fine, high windows so that the effect of this or that material, as it would be in a woman's dress, can be studied . . .

Tiny signposts like this show us vividly the way things have changed and remind us that even the most mundane of things that we take for granted, were new and startling once!

Nothing sold was branded, packed, standardized, or priced and customers had always to be on the watch, for shopping was a risky business. The price of everything had to be haggled about and settled by argument; and even when a price was finally agreed, the matter of actual payment could lead to further trouble. Daniel Defoe, writing in *The Compleat English Tradesman* in 1727, referred to a shortage of silver coinage and

33 Satirical engraving on the effects of beer. Notice the fishwife, and the man pawning his goods for a drink

to the frequent counterfeiting of money. So many coins were broken or filed down that customers were often asked to put their cash onto the scales and to make up any shortage of weight.

One result of all these difficulties was that credit was freely given in most shops and all customers, except the very poorest, were allowed to run up bills for as long as a year. Sometimes customers thought the charges too high and might refuse to pay in full, like Mrs Piozzi, Dr Johnson's friend, who was dissatisfied with Gillow's bill for furnishing her house, Streatham Park, and knocked £300 off the amount.

The idea of cash sales at fixed prices took a long time to

34　A coffee house at the beginning of the eighteenth century

develop. In 1750, a Mr Palmer opened a haberdashery shop on London Bridge and sold his goods at fixed prices; no bargaining was allowed, for each item was marked with its price on a little ticket. Fortunately for us, Mr Palmer took an apprentice aged fifteen who, fifty years later, described the shop in his auto-biography, *The Life of Robert Owen, by Himself*:

> It was a house established, and I believe the first, to sell at small profit and for ready money only . . . Not much time was allowed for bargaining, a price being fixed for everything and, compared with other houses, cheap. If any demur was made or much hesitation, the article asked for was withdrawn and another customer attended to.

Many people liked this new idea and flocked to Mr Palmer's shop as soon as it opened at eight o'clock in the morning, and had to be turned out when it closed at eleven at night. Goods were arranged in different departments and this, too, was a new convenience for customers. But, not surprisingly, Palmer was not popular with other shop-keepers, many of whom preferred to deal slowly and individually with their customers. His example was not followed for nearly a hundred years.

An eighteenth-century bookseller, John Dunton, wrote an autobiography in which he referred to some 150 booksellers in London and 300 in the country towns. The educated public was reading more and more and books were scarce. The letters of country gentlemen are full of requests to friends to buy particular books if they came across them.

Bookshops then were very different from those of today. The booksellers were the publishers; it was they who employed the printers and commissioned authors and in their shops their goods lay about unbound or were pinned up in loose sheets. If a customer liked the look of these he could sit down in the shop and read on the spot, on stools provided for the purpose. If he wished he could buy loose sheets and have them bound privately, or he could order a book from the bookseller, to be bound for him. Sometimes title pages were stuck up on the walls to be used as advertisement; later these might be given away to the 'dropping trade', to passers by; unsuccessful sheets were sold off to grocers for use as wrapping paper, or to cookshops to make pie-cases.

There was a flourishing second-hand book trade in London and dealers here, too, encouraged customers to drop in and browse and they would put half-read books aside until the next visit. There were no travelling libraries but many booksellers acted virtually as such. Here is a letter written in July 1694:

For my Worthy Friend, Mr John Dunton, Bookseller, at the Raven in the Poultry, London
Sir,
 I have taken notice of the second volume of the French book of Martyrs, and when your man comes my way I shall be glad if he will bring me one to read for a week. If I keep it a day longer (Provided he then calls upon me for itt) or if there be the least damage done to it, I shall be content to pay for the book.
I wish you health and happiness and am,
Your very humble servant

[Sir Peter Pett]

Abraham Dent of Kirby Stephen sold almanacs, magazines, and books among grocery, mercery, wines, patent medicines, and gunpowder. *Old Moore's* almanac was a perennial favourite and five different magazines were regularly bought and circulated among families and friends: *The London, The Universal, The*

35 A milliner's shop, 1789. These extravagant fashions were only for the wealthy

Royal, The Gentlemen's, and *The Beauties of all the Magazines selected.*

The bad state of the roads still isolated many towns from one another and made the carriage of goods difficult and risky. Parcels and light packets could be carried by coach along the main roads, and across country by strings of packhorses. Because of the risk of breakage, delay, and even loss, manufacturers made all the use they could of water transport. Coal came to the south by sea from Northumberland and Durham and – an extreme example of a devious route – the Horsehay Company, near Wellington in Shropshire, was sending pig iron to Chester by carting it to the Severn, putting it on river-boats to Bristol, and then onto ships sailing round the coast of Wales and up the Dee to Chester – a journey of over 400 miles by water, with two trans-shipments of cargo, to avoid one of 60 miles by land!

London had almost complete supremacy in matters of taste and, in spite of transport difficulties, well-to-do country families often still arranged for many of their requirements to be bought for them in the capital by an agent or by a carrier. There is frequent mention, in eighteenth-century letters, of carriers bringing special foodstuffs, snuff, fine materials for making clothes and curtains, and new furniture.

Mrs Purefroy, of Shalstone in Buckinghamshire, wrote to London on 6 February 1747:

Mr Willson,
I desire you will send mee
One pound of the best Bohea Tea
Half a pound of the best Green Tea
Two pounds of the best Coffeeberries [sic]
A quarter of a pound of nutmegs
Two ounces of mace
A quarter of an hundred of the best treble refined loaf sugar
A quarter of an hundred of Household sugar about 6 pence a pound
Half a quarter of an hundred of Rice
Send these by ye Buckingham carrier . . . send your Bill with them and will order you payment. The last Bohea tea was so ordinary I could not drink it, my neighbours had as good for six shillings a pound. The last hundredweight of Raisins you send were so bad they spoiled the Liquor they were made on. I hope you will send no more bad Goods, I have had no reason to complain till now, tho' I have dealt at yr shop these forty years and am
                              Your humble serft

                                                              E.P.
P.S. If you can't conveniently send them on Tuesday Mr Jones ye carrier sets out of London on Saturday mornings early.

Many people were reluctant to trust craftsmen in local towns to repair their valuables. Mr Purefroy sent his watch to London when it needed mending and another Buckinghamshire land-owner even packed his harpsichord in a load of hay and sent it to London to be tuned! But a Mrs Hawthorn was confident enough to put this notice in the Newcastle Courant of 13 February 1779:

M. Hawthorn, Widow of the late John Hawthorn, Watchmaker of this town, tenders her grateful thanks to the friends of her late husband; and begs to acquaint them and the public, that she will carry on the said Business (having engaged able workmen therein) and hopes for the continuance of their favours, which she will at all times studiously endeavour to merit.
Jewelry, Trinkets, Watches, Music and Musical Instruments.

And many fashionable London hairdressers left their premises in the Strand and migrated to country towns to dress customers' hair during race-meetings, when the assizes were held, or at any other festive time.

The would-be purchaser of fine new mahogany furniture could discover what was available by looking through such catalogues and guides as Thomas Chippendale's *The Gentleman and Cabinet-Maker's Director* (1754), and *The Universal System of Household Furniture* by William Ince and Thomas Mayhew (*c* 1762), both of which contained scores of illustrated items, from canopy beds to china shelves. Shortly after the death of George Hepplewhite in 1786, the company carried on by his widow issued *The Cabinet-Maker and Upholsterer's Guide*.

But while these books are valuable evidence to us about what was available to eighteenth-century families wishing to renew their household furnishings, none of the drawings are as vivid as a glimpse of the pieces in their original setting. For information about most of what was bought and sold at that time we have to rely upon written evidence, but in the case of furniture we can consult those early substitutes for the modern camera – the painters who captured daily life in innumerable 'Conversation' pieces and provided legacies of information that could have been handed down in no other way.

When Sophie de la Roche was in the Haymarket, London, she 'witnessed a method of taking hay to market which aroused my admiration and caused me no little pleasure', but she did not, on that occasion, make any mention of the shops. She must have passed a snuff shop which had already stood there for over fifty years, and which is still in the Haymarket today. This shop, Fribourg and Treyer's, was founded in 1720 in what was then a new and fashionable shopping area. Some elegant houses had been built in the streets nearby, so there was nowhere convenient for Mr Fribourg to graze his horse when he rode in from his home in the village of Ealing, some 6 miles away. He led her up the steps and through the shop and stabled her in the little yard behind!

Mr Fribourg the 'Snuffman' was a very strict employer and insisted that his assistants should do exactly what he wanted in the way he wanted. Here are the *Regulations for Staff* which everybody who worked there had to learn by heart and obey:

36 Typical eighteenth-century shop front, still in use today

A few rules requisite to be observed in the care and management of a Shop:

1. Open the shop at six o'clock in the summer, and as soon as it is light in the winter, clean it and put all things in their proper places.
2. Enter all orders as soon as you receive them in the Order Book and compare the entry with the Order
3. Let every order be dispatched as soon as possible if by Coach or by Waggon the first after receipt of your order. Clean the Counter of everything before you put up an order, for fear

37 London Bridge with its shops, from an engraving by Visscher

other articles be packed with it, and sent wrong; always restore all goods to their proper situations after serving a Customer.

4. Pack up no parcel or other Article till it be first entered in the Waste Book or Journal and carefully called over.

5. Always make out the Bill of Parcels from the Book and not from the Articles.

6. Compare the Bill of Parcels with the Book and cast up the Bill and the Book separately, which will discover if there be any mistake.

7. All goods received are to be examined by the Bill of Parcels as soon as they are opened; if there be no Bill, take an account of the particulars and compare it when you receive one.

8. Never leave the Shop without one of the Family in it.

9. Desire all strangers that enquire for the Governor in his absence to leave their Names and Businesses if agreeable and immediately enter it in the Order or Minute Book that your memory may be neither burthened nor trusted.

10. Leave no Book of Accounts open in any public place; and always clean the Counter of everything which is not in use.

11. Never omit any Business till to Morrow if it can as well be done to day, for no one knows, what the Morrow may bring forth.

Go to the ant, consider her ways and be wise;
Banish sloth, and the inordinate love of ease;
The hand of the diligent maketh rich
Active minds only are fit for Business.
Remember!! none but the strictly honest, industrious and
trustworthy can possibly thrive, nor can they obtain or
deserve a good name which, as Solomon wisely and truly
says, is rather to be chosen than great riches.

Many writers of the time referred to the high standard of
behaviour expected of tradesmen. Defoe, in *The Compleat
Tradesman* explained that a tradesman 'must never be angry,
not so much as seen to be so, if a customer tumbles him £100
worth of goods and scarce bid for anything'. And *The London
Tradesman* of 1747 laid down further qualifications for a successful shop-keeper in a fashionable district:

He ought to speak fluently, though not elegantly, to entertain the
ladies; and to be master of a handsome bow and cringe; should be
able to hand a lady to and from her coach politely, without
being seized with a palpitation of the heart at the touch of a
delicate hand, the sight of a well-turned and much exposed limb,
or a handsome face.

38   Cheapside, in London. Notice the cobbled streets,
shop signs and bollards to separate off the pedestrians

Apprentices had to do the same work as the older assistants but had to start work earlier. There were no laws at all about working conditions and Robert Owen, writing fifty years later, gives us a glimpse of his boyhood work in the haberdashery on London Bridge:

> . . . up and had breakfasted and was dressed to receive customers in the shop at eight o'clock; – and dressing then was no slight affair. Boy as I was then, I had to wait my turn for the hair-dresser to powder and pomatum and curl my hair, for I had two large curls at each side, and a stiff pigtail, and until all this was very nicely and systemically done, no-one could think of appearing before a customer. Between eight and nine o'clock the shop began to fill with purchasers, and their number increased until it was crowded to excess, although a large apartment, and this continued until late in the evening; usually until ten or half past ten, during all the spring months. Dinner and tea were hastily taken, two or three, sometimes only one, escaping at a time to take what he or she could the most easily swallow and returning to take the places of others who were serving. But when the purchasers left at ten or half past ten, before the shop could be quite clear a new part of the business was to be commenced. The articles dealt in as haberdashery were innumerable, and these when exposed to the customers were tossed and tumbled and unfolded in the utmost confusion and disorder, and there was no time or space to put anything right and in order during the day. This was a work to be performed with closed doors after the customers had been shut out at eleven o'clock; and it was often two o'clock in the morning before the goods in the shop had been put in order and replaced to be ready for the next day's similar proceedings. Frequently at two o'clock in the morning, after being actively engaged on foot all day from eight o'clock in the morning, I have scarcely been able with the aid of the banisters to go upstairs to bed. And then I had but about five hours for sleep.

Fairs were still important in eighteenth-century England and among the largest were those specializing in the sale of cattle and sheep. At Howden, in Yorkshire, the Great Fair was at this time the largest in the country and offered large flocks of sheep for sale to butchers, as well as horses for carriers, coaching companies, and the army. Apart from cattle and sheep fairs there were others which were really glorified markets, offering every conceivable commodity for sale.

Defoe described Sturbridge Fair as:

39   Buying laces and flounces, 1777

. . . not only the greatest in the nation, but in the world. . . . The
shops are placed in rows like streets, whereof one is called Cheapside; and here . . . are all sorts of trades, who sell by retale, and
who come principally from London with their goods; scarce any
trades are omitted, goldsmiths, toyshops, brasiers, turners,
milleners, haberdashers, hatters, mercers, drapers, pewtrers,
china-warehouses . . . with coffee-houses, taverns, brandy shops,
and eating houses innumerable, and all in tents and booths as
above. . . . In a word, the fair is like a well fortyfy'd city, and there
is the least disorder and confusion (I believe) that can be seen
anywhere, with so great a concourse of people.

Most of the traders at fairs catered mainly for the general
public but some offered bargains to local shop-keepers. A
London dealer at Bury Fair, in Lancashire, during October
1763 announced:

Jones, wholesale linen factors, will open a warehouse during the
time of the fair, when he will have a large number of linen-
drapery goods, and for the sake of ready money will dispose of

the same to country shop-keepers at least twopence in the yard cheaper than they would have them by giving their orders to any House in London.

Improvements in transport gradually lessened farmers' dependence on nearby fairs, and as more shops opened in every town, fewer people found it to their advantage to shop at fairs. Increasingly, the bad character of some of those selling there, and the drunken and disorderly behaviour of the crowds caused annoyance to local residents and many fairs were closed down.

The beginnings of factory production in the midlands and the north of England produced such a wide variety of goods that many manufacturers began to think of new ways of disposing of their products. At about the turn of the century wholesale travelling dealers, popularly called 'Manchester men', began to carry goods from the new factories to shop-keepers up and down the country. They were not pedlars, though they did sometimes sell direct to customers.

Their rivals, in a sense, were the Scotch Drapers, travelling retailers who called on foot from house to house and sold on credit, mainly to poor families in isolated districts. In the early years of industrialization, when new mills, factories, and mines were isolated in valleys in the north, the Scotch Draper brought to their door the type of new, cheap goods that people welcomed but could not get locally.

So for the poor as well as for the rich, for townsmen and countrymen, for northerners as well as southerners, the final years of the eighteenth century brought increasing availability of material goods, and greater opportunities of acquiring improvements for home and family. Dreadful inequalities there still were, and would be for very much longer, but things that had been rarities a century before were becoming common-places and luxuries were, for some people, becoming necessities. It is significant to the theme of this book that virtually all the extra goods made and consumed came from *outside* the home and entailed more shopping to make life more comfortable and satisfying.

6 The Nineteenth Century

UNTIL THE COMING of the railways in the first half of the nineteenth century, the country housewife was faced with the same
difficulties and the same anxieties about her domestic supplies
as her predecessors had been. She had to cater for enormous
numbers and gargantuan appetites and although more foods
were gradually available to her, more was demanded as the
standard of living slowly rose. She grew what she could and had
to make a special journey, perhaps every three months, to buy
other supplies in the nearest market town.

But the 'iron horse' distributed goods widely and quickly
and made shopping and catering much easier in both town and
country. There was great impetus given to the use of fresh fish,
for example, and it is from about 1850 that we can date the
decline in popularity of salted and pickled herrings, which had
for centuries been one of the chief foods available to people
living inland. Oysters, too, had for long been so cheap that they
were within the purse of everybody but the very poorest. As
late as 1840 they cost only 4d a dozen, but within a few years
they were so expensive that only the wealthy could afford them.
This rise in the status of the oyster was caused by reckless
dredging of the natural beds to meet increasing demand from
the rapidly expanding towns.

Victorian cookery books describe a wide variety of new recipes
for fish dishes. Mrs Isabella Beeton's *Book of Household Management*,
first published in 1861, gives advice about marketing for this,
that, and the other, and the author seems to have taken it for
granted that her readers would be able to buy everything they
needed. In her books nobody grows food, hunts it, or makes it;
she is the first townswoman's cookery adviser.

In the latter part of Queen Victoria's reign many people
were beginning to enjoy moderate comfort for the first time.
Goods of many kinds were coming into the shops in quantities
much greater and at prices lower than ever before, and
earnings – for those fortunate enough to have regular jobs –
were improving. The range of fruit and vegetables available
to the town housekeeper was considerable. Most was still grown
in Britain, but increasing amounts came from abroad and

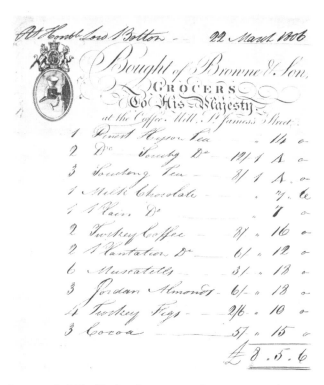

40 A grocer's bill. Notice how expensive tea must have been. It was not a drink for everyone

during the 1860s there are constant references, for example, in the journals of Bristol merchants, to the departure of emigrant ships for Australia and their return with cargoes of Australian products. The English farmer might be impoverished by imported cheap meat and grain, but the English town housewife had very good reason to be glad of it.

Watercress, and most of the herbs sold in Covent Garden, were still supplied by women who gathered them wild in the countryside. Dandelions, scurvy-grass, bittersweet, feverfew, red valerian, and hedge mustard were sold by itinerant country women or at stalls in the open markets.

William Home's *The Table Book*, published in 1898, refers to grapes being available in the shops and markets from the

41 Street of houses where shop fronts have been added

middle of June to the middle of November, 'but dear'. Cherries
were the Biggarreau or Graffion, and also the black or Dutch
Guigne type; pears were English Kargonelle, Windsor and
Green Chisel; apples were mainly Dutch codlin, Carlisle
codlin, Jenneting, Summer Pearmain, and Hawthornden.
The very names have a flavour.

There were no laws about keeping foodstuffs fresh and
during the first half of the century much of the food sold was
often seriously adulterated. In 1830 a young chemist, named
Accum, published a *Treatise on the Adulteration of Food and
Culinary Poisons* which caused a sensation. Many of the adultera-
tions which Accum exposed had been practised for many years –
alum was put into bread to whiten it, lead into cider and

93

wine, plaster of Paris into flour, chalk into milk, capsicum into mustard, and so on. It appears that Gloucester cheese was often coloured with red lead, and confectionery coloured by the use of highly poisonous salts of both lead and copper. In 1824 a Mr Tatham of Golden Square in London informed a magistrate that he and his family and a party of friends were taken seriously ill after eating coloured 'wafer cakes' bought from 'a respectable shop', and when the cakes were analysed they were found to contain verdigris and sugar of lead.

F. W. Hackwood, the author of *Good Cheer*, published in 1911 reported:

> A curious case of adulteration [was] revealed in evidence given at court a century ago, which discovered that many persons made a living by picking sloe-leaves and whitethorn-leaves in the fields near Camberwell, and selling them to a local cowkeeper for a penny a pound. One man said he picked from fifty to sixty pounds a day, and always found a market for them. The leaves were subsequently sold to a wholesale merchant, who could obtain as much as 8s a pound for them under the guise of tea. The merchant was prosecuted and fined, not for adulteration, but for defrauding the Revenue. And the 'tea-leafer' is still the slang name for the petty thief.

The quality of the milk supplied to townspeople was still unbelievably bad, and though the development of the railways made it possible to bring country milk into the towns, most of London's milk continued to be supplied by cows kept in half-underground cellars, such as these in Golden Square, described in 1847:

> Forty cows are kept in them, two in each seven feet of space. There is no ventilation, save by the unceiled tile roof, through which the ammoniacal vapours escape . . . Besides the animals, there is at one end a large tank for grains, a storeplace for turnips and hay, and between them a receptacle into which the liquid manure drains, and the solid is heaped . . . the stench thus arising is insufferable.

Watering milk and removing the fat were very common practices, and no thinking mother could have felt happy about the milk she bought, either in town or country, though of course nothing was known about bacterial infection until the work of Pasteur became accepted. It was not until about 1890

42   London dustman, from Pyne's *Costumes of Great Britain*. The profits from scavenging were so great that dustmen were unpaid and competed for contracts

that pasteurization began to be used in a few more progressive parts of the dairy industry.

The state of the meat markets in the poorer parts of nineteenth-century towns was little better than it had been in the Middle Ages and there was much concern at the deaths thought to be caused by diseased meat. At a time when ordinary butchers' meat was particularly dear, an attempt was made to introduce the trade in horse-meat, which was already very successful in Paris. But British people had for long had a special relationship with horses and would not, knowingly, eat them.

Punch and *The Lancet* were foremost in their denunciation of the widespread malpractices. In 1851 *Punch* published a series of articles entitled 'Sermons to Tradesmen', in which there were scathing descriptions of the 'imps' who infested the food trade:

> Imps of all trades were there. The Baker-Imp who grinds his alum to make his bread; and selling the staff of life, makes the staff carry a mischievous weapon for the bowels of him who trusts to it.

95

43   A patent 'modesty machine' for fitting the ladies!

The Grocer-Imp who enriches his chocolate with brick-dust; and with a morning draught conveys the materials of a vault. The Milk-man Imp with chalk against customer, and chalk inside him.

The Confectioner-Imp, who paints Twelfth Cakes with emerald green (a beautiful change for coppers, in an arsenite development) and – especially in holiday times – plays HEROD among the innocents.

The Publican-Imp, whose head of beer is green copperas – whose ale is sharpened with the fiery edges of vitriol, and whose grains-of-paradise are gifts of the serpent.[1]

As a result of protests and denunciations, a Select Parliamentary Commission was appointed to consider the whole question of food adulteration and, in 1860, the first Food and Drugs Act was passed. This was a well-intentioned measure, which authorized county authorities to appoint analysts to control the quality of foodstuffs offered for sale, but it was

[1] *Punch*, 1851, Vol XX

administered in a half-hearted fashion, largely because of opposition from traders. Consumer interests gradually made themselves heard with greater emphasis however and in 1872 the Act was drastically amended, the appointment of shop inspectors was made compulsory and from that date the identification and suppression of the food adulterator began to be more effective.

All social effort takes time to materialize, however, as we are reminded by this astonishing note which appeared in *The Chemist and Druggist* of 15 January 1876:

RECLAIMING BUTTER

A startling report has been published by the Glasgow News, disclosing some almost incredible facts in relation to the butter trade. The journal named met with a trade circular, some time back, issued to reclaim old butter, removing any taste of tallow, grease, and also bad smells, etc., at the same time slightly increasing the weight, at the rate of 7s. 6d. per cwt. if in casks, or 10s. 6d. cwt. if in Irish lumps. 'Any kind of old butter out of condition', said the circular, 'and heated qualities made suitable for table use again, and it becomes quite firm.'

It was not only country people whose shopping opportunities were widening, now that the railways enabled them to go 'to town' much more easily. In the bigger towns customers could get quickly from one district to another by the new horse omnibuses, and so could compare prices here and there before deciding to buy.

Improvements in the streets, no longer full of deep ruts breaking ankles and axles, led to a multiplication of vehicles: light curricles, phaetons, hackney-carriages, had replaced the lumbering coaches. But streets paved with stone were noisy, those macadamized were muddy; either way they were still dangerous to pedestrians. All blended with the vocal pattern of London, its air clamorous with the cries of flower-sellers, crossing-sweepers, shoe-blacks, chimney-sweeps, herbalists, match-sellers, baked-potato men, sellers of hot bread, and costermongers. Henry Mayhew, in *London Labour and the London Poor*, reported that the street-sellers all kept to their own line of business.

There was an exciting increase in the number and variety of shops. The 1891 census showed an increase of 40 per cent, since 1881, in the numbers of green-grocers, grocers, fish-

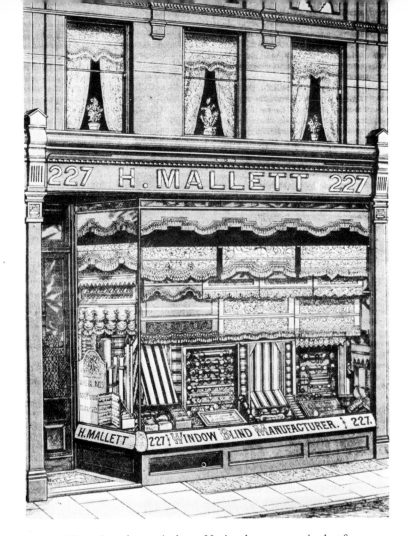

44 A Victorian shop window. Notice how every inch of space has been filled

mongers, and other traders in food. Many new kinds of more or less specialized kinds of shops were being opened and the old type of general shop-keeper gradually became scarcer. More and more people were employed in making machinery which served the everyday needs of the ordinary family. Machinery for boot-making and for the garment trades, for example, brought down the prices of footwear and clothing and Charles Booth, with all his knowledge of the appalling handicaps against which the poor had to struggle, could say of the working man and his family that: '. . . clothes necessary for comfort are usually good and suitable . . . they wear well and are well worn . . . as a rule, none of the clothes are second-hand.' The well-to-do might sneer at 'reach me downs' – ready-made garments which the shopman would 'reach down' from his shelf – but they were warm, respectable, and cheap.

Because of so much increasing trade, there began to be much more competition between shops, and a shop-keeper who wanted to prosper could no longer rely solely upon his regular customer coming to him. He had to think of attracting new ones.

One way of doing this was to fit larger windows. A shop in Ludgate Hill, in London, was the first to be fitted with windows reaching up to the first floor level, and gradually more and more shopfronts were enlarged. An article in *Chambers Journal* in 1864 described the new London shop-fronts:

> They form one of the most prominent indications of the grandeur and wealth of the metropolis. Enormous plate-glass windows, gilded or polished brass frames, expensive mirrors, polished mahogany frames and all sorts of fancy woodwork; sometimes crystal columns, and generally a singular covering of iron Venetian blinds, which roll up and down by intricate machinery, like a stage curtain displaying or concealing the gorgeous scenery within – these are the necessary decorations of a fashionable London shop.

The new, more tempting shops were stocked with the rapidly increasing factory products, and industry, in turn, was stimulated by the vast amount of new items displayed for passers-by to buy. Lady Violet Greville, in *Faiths and Fashions*, written in the 1880s, referred to the demand for:

> the numberless lace trifles, gaudy ribbons, satins, delicate frills and confections and headdresses, and whatever all the names may be of the various articles that sparkle and dangle and shine and attract in the plate-glass squares that make the delight of ladies' eyes!

Special attention was paid to 'carriage customers' who, supposedly casting lustre on the shops they patronized, were always received with special politeness.

45   Sunrise Store Wyoming, one of the early big general
stores. Notice the variety of goods on display

Enterprising shopkeepers began to change the lettering, too,
on their shopfronts, from the traditional elegant engraving on
brass, or gilt lettering on polished wood, to ornate glass or
porcelain letters, or carved and gilded ones. Here is a description of some of the new lettering over London shopfronts in
the middle of the century:

Some are very thick and short; some thin and lofty; some have
thick strokes where they ought to be thin, and vice versa; some
are represented perspectively, as if standing one behind another
like a file of soldiers; some follow each other vertically up the
front of the house; and in one instance that we have seen, the
letters are placed upside down.

A writer describing London in the 1840s referred to a new
kind of shop lighting which had recently been introduced in

46 The Burlington Arcade, London: a new shopping centre for the well-to-do

some main streets. Rows of gas flares, fixed outside above the plate glass windows, gave a dazzling effect and customers inside did not have to combat the unpleasantness of gas fumes or falling smuts.

Passers-by were also encouraged to spend their money by new forms of advertising: posters put up on walls by 'external paperhangers', handbills distributed at random, and placards carried by men in 'sandwich boards' who made chaotic traffic conditions even worse.

In many shops an assistant could supplement his meagre wages by earning 'tinge' – commissions on the goods he sold. This system led, of course, to many abuses: there were assistants who prided themselves on selling goods to customers at prices higher than those marked; others pestered customers and would not let them go without buying something, as a draper writing in 1876 about his work tells:

> Many a half-frightened girl have I seen go out of the shop, her purchase in her hands, the tears welling up in her eyes, shaking her head and saying 'I am sure I shall never like it' – some shawl or dress having been forced upon her contrary to her taste or judgement.

Reference is made in the early 1840s to the practice of 'ticketing' goods. In the window an article was shown at a bargain price; the customer was given an inferior article in the shop, but in the dim light the difference was not noticed. In many shops, assistants were encouraged to sell damaged or old stock at the same price as new goods. In 1861 there was formed an 'Association for Suppressing the Practice of Falsely Labelling Goods for Sale'; members were manufacturers and traders who aimed to prevent open fraud. That such an association was needed is illustrated by the following, in a book published in the same year:

> The British merchant has been found guilty of selling pieces of calico, nominally thirty-six yards in length, never measuring more than thirty yards. He is found guilty of selling thirty-six inches of silk lace, and calling it fifty-four inches . . . He is found guilty of increasing the weight of the hogshead, compared with the sugar it contains, from twelve per cent of the gross weight to seventeen per cent . . . He is found guilty of pirating designs, of imitating the wrappers of well-known makers, and of forging popular trade marks . . . He is found guilty of reducing the weight of candles (sold in bunches) until the buyer is defrauded of two ounces in his pound . . . These frauds are all considered, by those who practise and grow rich on them, as allowable customs of the trade.

It was not only shop-keepers who were sometimes dishonest, but customers too. There is a curious modern ring about a ballad, *Ladies, Don't go Thieving*, which was hawked about London streets in 1867:

> . . . A beauty to the West End went,
> Around a shop she lingers,
> And there upon some handkerchiefs
> She clapped her pretty fingers.
> Into the shop she gently popped,
> The world is quite deceiving
> When ladies have a notion got
> To ramble out a-thieving . . .

Of course voluminous skirts were a help in hiding stolen goods and in 1885 a crinolined lady was caught with 24½ yards of velvet, 42 silk handkerchiefs, 2 pairs of gloves, and some ribbons, all hidden on her person! For such offences severe sentences often amounting to several months' hard labour were imposed on conviction.

We can read vivid descriptions of shop life in the novels of H. G. Wells and his contemporaries. In *The History of Mr Polly* and in *Kipps* the conditions are grim indeed, but this is not, by itself, reliable history and needs to be read alongside the many diaries and reports on conditions in nineteenth-century shops.

47 A London coffee stall, by Holman Hunt. Tea and coffee had become more popular drinks by the end of the nineteenth century

The living-in system was general, developed from the earlier arrangements under which the apprentice was one of the master's family. Once trade reached a certain level and the number of apprentices and assistants became larger than a family, an institutional atmosphere was inevitable. The quality

48 A draper's assistant. Notice the obsequiously humble expression which he has been taught to assume

of the life of those employed depended, of course, upon the humanity of the shop-keeper. There were, as there always are, good employers and bad ones and it was pure luck that landed you with this one or that. For a very long time society took little interest and eschewed any suggestion of control. It is interesting that working hours and conditions in factories were matters of public concern and parliamentary action more than half a century earlier than those in shops. There is no equivalent to Thomas Hood's *Song of the Shirt* to draw attention to conditions in shops. A writer in 1843 reported that drapers' assistants work:

> from six, seven or eight o'clock in the morning, to nine, ten, eleven or twelve o'clock in the evening; the variations being according to the season, the character of the shop, and the custom of the neighbourhood. Shops are open longer in summer than in winter, those catering for the middle and working classes are open longer than those serving the upper classes.

A minimum amount of space was provided for the assistants and many had nothing more than a place to eat in common and a bed, or the share of a bed, in a crowded room. Because they were needed in the shop until late, sitting rooms for them were often thought unnecessary and often there were no conveniences on the premises. As Sunday was not a working day, the inmates of many establishments were expected to fend for themselves on that day and were shut out from 10 am until 9 or 10 in the evening. Many male assistants spent the day walking the streets, or in the public house; girls and women were often so exhausted that they spent most of the day in bed, when this was allowed. In either case the employer was displeased, for he liked his employees to appear at church because it looked more respectable and added to his reputation as an employer. Church services were, in fact, among the few opportunities of a free rest and sleep for over-tired employees with nowhere to go.

Shop employees could be dismissed without notice and often they were dismissed if they married, 'for it is considered an axiom that a married man is not so effective a salesman as one who is single', said a writer in 1854. When an assistant was ill, his salary stopped and he was expected to leave his bed to go to the dining room for meals, or to go without food. The 'fortnight's holiday with pay' was unheard of for shop assistants, and even without pay it was out of the question. *Punch* was still fighting for a Saturday half-holiday in the 1860s.

Early in the 1840s change was in the air, particularly in the industrial north. Liverpool and Manchester were excited by the agitation of the Chartists and the propaganda of the Anti-Corn Law League, in Rochdale some working men were planning what was to become the first successful co-operative shop, and even shop assistants were beginning to make public complaints against their conditions of work. An association of drapers' assistants was formed to work for a reduction in working hours and an article in the *Liverpool Monthly Magazine* appealed to its lady readers to patronize only those shops whose owners accepted the shorter working hours suggested by the association.

In 1842 the Early Closing Association was formed in London. Charles Dickens, always active on behalf of social causes, was one of the members and did a great deal, by his writings and speeches, to influence public opinion, and during the following decades many appeals were made to the public to abstain from shopping in the evening, so that employers would in time find it uneconomic to keep their shops open late. There were a great many people of goodwill who wrote, lectured, and campaigned on behalf of better hours for shop assistants. One writer urged:

> Let those of us who are living in affluence resolve to buy what articles we want during the first five and a half days of the week. Let us not buy anything after six in the evening. Let us enter no shop on a Saturday afternoon. Let us pay the wages of our workmen on Friday evening at the latest.

Probably the early closing of shops in better-class districts was mainly due to the fact that richer customers usually went home to dinner between six and seven in the evening, and ladies were not normally seen in the streets after that time. The working classes, on the other hand, did not get home until later, and probably found the brightly lit streets a welcome diversion.

There were innumerable small tradesmen who continued to keep their shops open very late on six days a week and who opened for half the day on Sunday. These effectively blocked progress, but so did two other factors: the general dislike of any interference in free market conditions and a feeling among many shop assistants themselves that they were socially superior to factory workers and did not need to be helped by legislation. However, our Victorian ancestors' strong social conscience certainly needed to be supported by legislation and the first Shop Hours Act of 1886 provided that no one under 18 years of age should work longer than a 74-hour week. This was a step forward, but adult workers were not affected by the Act and continued well into the present century to work desperately long hours.

In the mills he managed and inherited at New Lanark, Robert Owen not only looked after the working conditions of his employees, including such unheard-of amenities as a nursery school and a canteen, but he provided a special shop where his men could buy good things at a low price. This was run entirely without profit and gave some of Robert Owen's followers the idea of founding co-operative shops by means of the issue of £1 shares. The first co-operative shop was opened at Rochdale in 1844. The 'Rochdale Pioneers' supplied only the best goods, they allowed no credit as a matter of principle, gave full weight,

49　Fullers 'Temple of Fancy', an early nineteenth century gift shop selling luxury knick knacks

and divided the profits between members, by payment of a 'dividend'. The idea was highly successful and did much to make life tolerable for the poor and the unemployed.

Co-operative Societies were the first of the large-scale retailers to prosper, and they were inevitably attacked by small traders. In the 1860s *The Grocer*, the trade paper of the small shopkeeper, tried to organize a boycott among their readers of all wholesalers and manufacturers who supplied goods to the Co-op Retail Societies. But the Co-operative movement had an essentially ethical purpose. The word was used as an antithesis to 'competition' and co-operation was thought of as a principle of life, rather than a mere system of profitable shopping and storekeeping.

In London, fashionable people flocked to new shopping places called 'Bazaars': the Soho Bazaar, the Baker Street Bazaar, and the Pantheon Bazaar in Oxford Street. A Bazaar was a large building with stalls and open counters ranged on both sides of long passages on several different floors. Stalls were rented from the owner of the building. Here is a description of the Pantheon Bazaar in the middle of the century:

50   The Great Saloon of the Pantheon, Oxford Street, 1840

When we have passed through the entrance porch in Oxford
Street we find ourselves in a vestibule containing a few sculptures,
and from thence a flight of steps lead up, to a range of rooms
occupied as a picture gallery. These pictures are placed here for
sale, the proprietors of the bazaar receiving a commission or
percentage on any picture which may find a purchaser. From
these rooms an entrance is obtained to the top-bazaar, one of the
most tasteful places of the kind in London. We look down upon
the ground storey and find it arranged with counters loaded with
uncountable trinkets. On one counter are articles of millinery, on
another lace, on a third gloves and hosiery, on others cutlery,
jewellery, toys, children's dresses, books, sheets of music, albums,

51   Ladies in an elevator on the opening date at Lord and Taylor's Store, Broadway, 1872

porcelain ornaments, cut-glass ornaments, artificial flowers, feathers and a host of other things. Each counter is attended by a young female.

It was becoming increasingly the custom for families to leave London during the summer months and this had its effect upon shopkeepers. Charles Dickens was in London in September 1853 and wrote to a friend reporting how quiet everything was. He had called on two tailors of his acquaintance and found one playing the piano upstairs with his family, and the other had gone to Brighton. His hosier in New Bond Street was also away and the shop was in the charge of two young assistants who were playing draughts in the back parlour. Horizons were indeed changing . . .

A great impetus to trade was given by the Great Exhibition of 1851. The 'Crystal Palace' resembled a huge shop window whose wares had been contributed by the peoples of every country to show how they could serve one another. Over 6 million people, young and old, flocked to Hyde Park to see the Exhibition and many of these must have enquired where they could buy this, that, or the other. Many shopkeepers, too, as they walked round with their wives and children, must have noticed things they would like to stock in their shops if they had sufficient capital and space.

Initiative, imagination, and courage, too, were needed by any tradesman who thought of widening the scope of his traditional business and these were qualities possessed in considerable degree by one young man who visited the Exhibition. He was William Whiteley, an apprentice haberdasher from Yorkshire, whose whole life was changed by what he saw when he visited the Great Exhibition. He conceived the idea of owning a shop that would supply everything

52   A saddler's shop, Camberley. Goods were made, repaired and sold here

that a customer could want, all under one roof. This was a new and exciting idea.

Whiteley left Yorkshire and worked in a number of drapers' shops in London and so gained experience and accumulated a modest amount of capital. He chose very carefully the district in which to open a new haberdashery shop and this, in Westbourne Grove, a district on the fringe of the newly fashionable area of Bayswater, was an instantaneous success. His customers were never pestered to buy things they did not want; everything was displayed to the best advantage and marked in plain figures; all goods were sold at a reasonable profit and purchasers were never given any excuse for complaint.

Whiteley soon found his business growing; he engaged more and more staff, bought up a number of adjacent small shops and extended his business until Whiteley the draper became Whiteley the 'Universal Provider' as he called himself. We, today, are well accustomed to the idea of a 'store' but in the 1860s and 1870s it was unheard of and William Whiteley, while highly successful with his many customers, was criticized and disliked by small shopkeepers and others who were jealous of his success.

Whiteley did not advertise in the usual way in the newspapers; he believed in approaching his customers personally by circulars and thought too of a new method of publicity. He issued to his customers *Whiteley's Diary and Almanac for 1877*, a completely new departure in shop-keeping. In the 1878 Almanac he announced a delivery system which was a marvel of efficiency: every day the London householder could rely upon two regular deliveries by special van and the suburban householder upon one, country customers could have goods sent free of charge by train or, if necessary, by express coach; foreign customers, too, were well served and Whiteley's goods became known all over the world. Whiteley's success inevitably caused others to imitate his methods and it is no exaggeration to say that he changed the whole pattern of shopkeeping in Britain.

The idea of a 'department store' was, at the same time, being put into operation in the United States by A. T. Stewart, whose vast shop in New York employed 2,000 people and sold a wide assortment of manufactured articles. But New York was not

53   Part of Fifth Avenue, New York City in 1902

America, then any more than now; imported luxuries did not penetrate in quantity into the western hinterland until the railroads were built and marketing grew on a national scale.

With the rapid extension of the railroad network across the continent, merchants tended to make fewer journeys to buy their stock, but began to be served by travelling salesmen. A firm in Waterbury, Connecticut, made a pioneering experiment in the 1830s, in sending out a button salesman to the Middle West. He was not a pedlar, but had already many of the characteristics of the modern commercial traveller. He carried no stock with him, but sold only from sample cards; he did not accept 'barter goods', but took orders and the company made delivery later by freight.

Faster communications caused a new profusion of goods to appear in the country stores. Every year brought new wonders: gaslight in the cities, kerosene lamps in the country, ready-made shirts, barbed-wire fencing, screens to keep the flies out, the magnetic telegraph, gun-cotton, chloroform, a printing press that could roll off 10,000 newspapers in an hour, new stuff called 'celluloid', and, as the century wore on, pianolas, gramophones, and chewing gum.

Nearly every country store had a patent medicine shelf beside the cattle powders and poultry remedies, and sales were brisk. Whatever effect the medicines had upon public health, their packaging contributed greatly to the prosperity of paper mills, printing, and engraving shops, glassworks, box factories, magazines, and newspapers.

The patent medicine makers supplemented their advertising in the newspapers by using an old American institution, which William Whiteley was to copy in London – the almanac. These were small, printed booklets giving information of every conceivable kind: when to plant and reap this, that, and the other, letter postage rates, stage routes, the dates of eclipses, and so on were mixed in with bits of poetry and history, moral precepts, sentimental tales, and, gradually, advertisements for medicines of all kinds. *Boston Almanac* for the year 1841 included a novelty – a complete 'Business Directory' – a list of all business people and firms in the city, alphabetically arranged under each occupation. There were forty-three different categories: West India goods and retail groceries took up four and a half columns, wholesale groceries 2 columns, merchants 2 columns, described as 'principally ship owners, and importers of cargoes of Russia [sic], S. American, Calcutta, Canton, European, and W. Indian Goods etc.' Such almanacs reached isolated communities thirsty for information and diversion and gave them a sense of belonging to the rapidly changing outside world.

A regular supplier was the 'essence pedlar', described by Nathaniel Hawthorne in his *American Notes*:

His essences were of aniseed, cloves, red cedar, wormwood, together with opodeldoc and an oil for the hair . . . Cologne waters is among the essences manufactured, tho' the bottles have foreign labels on them . . . This man was a pedlar in quite a small way, and carrying no more than an open basket full of essences, but some go out with wagon loads.

Nowhere was too remote for the pack-pedlar. In 1850 there were 10,669 on the road in the United States and in 1860 there

54 Warehouses on the London Docks. Notice the air of grimness and overcrowding

55 A hawker demonstrates the value of his rat-traps

were 16,600. In many states they had to be licensed, to keep control of the 'foreign goods' – goods from other states – that they sold. There were even women-pedlars, many of them Syrian or Armenian, selling lace, doilies, pins, needles, thread, and cheap jewellery. All these, and the cobblers, spinners, tailors, silhouette-cutters, portrait-painters, and others who travelled the roads brought gossip, news, goods and services to even the most remote homesteads. But peddling dropped off during the Civil War and did not pick up again, as railroads brought people nearer to markets and stores.

Goods arriving in bulk in country stores had for long been 'branded'. In its original meaning a brand was a mark applied with a blacking brush or a hot iron to a bale or cask, showing where the contents came from or who had shipped them. A brand was also a mark put on a container as a sign that the contents had been examined and passed by a public inspector, and so it came to mean a grade or a certain quality. Buyers came to recognize the brand marks and to rely on them.

By the 1860s a few articles were ready-wrapped in amounts convenient for the buyer and the wrapper was printed as an identifying label. In addition the name, or brand, was sometimes impressed on the actual goods – such as the words 'American Family' on a bar of soap.

Between the 1860s and 1880s many factories began to pack their goods in small quantities wrapped in paper and one could buy 'a paper' of coffee, a 'paper' of dried yeast, and so on. The papers were for the convenience of the purchaser, but they began to be used as advertisements and before long thicker paper and even card were being used for wrapping. This idea of packaging quickly became popular and new ways developed. Boots and shoes used to be tumbled helter skelter into a wooden bin; later they were delivered to the store with twelve pairs in a carton; and finally each pair had a box of its own.

In the 1880s the old methods of book-keeping began to change too. The first cash register ever used in a general store was installed at Coalton, Ohio, in 1879 and registers were soon widely used. They saved time, work, and book-keeping and removed the temptation for clerks to pocket small sums on the side.

Both in Britain and in the USA the vigorous advertising campaigns and the attractive trading methods of the leading stores led to a rapid rise in their popularity with shoppers. Existing stores enlarged their buildings and the range of goods and services provided, and other retailers began to raise capital for expansion by converting their businesses into limited companies.

But some people learned from experience that the new department stores were not necessarily the best places to shop economically. Mrs M. V. Hughes, the wife of a young London barrister wrote in *A London Home in the Nineties*:

> Bessie . . . had advised me to get everything at Whiteley's. 'You've only got to walk into the shop, order what you want in the different departments, and you find everything delivered at your door'. She was right, but I soon found that this easy way of buying had to be paid for by too high prices, so I determined to explore the neighbourhood, buy what I wanted and bring it home myself.

Mrs Hughes discovered, in the same area as Whiteleys, shops and stalls selling fresh foods at reasonable prices:

One shop, a greengrocer's, was the most satisfactory place of business I have ever been in . . . The premises were allowed to remain ramshackle, no books were kept, no credit given, and the whole energy of the staff was devoted to getting the best they could every morning from Covent Garden and selling it quickly at a small profit. By the 'best' I don't mean exotic fruits, but great piles of what was 'in', served out to the first comers (often little children) with good humour, homely manners, and very little wrapping up. Once I had already filled my shopping basket when I spied some sprouts and begged for a paper bag to put them in. 'Not for greens, my dear' was the inexorable reply.

56   A label for Gold Leaf tobacco, c 1870, with a 'western' motif

7 The Twentieth Century

IN MANY WAYS the nineteenth century did not really end until 1914. Britain was still 'two nations' as Disraeli had described it in 1845: well-to-do families lived elegantly, with an army of servants to wait upon them, but there was an enormous amount of poverty and misery among the poor.

The family tradition of shop-keeping was declining; the combined shop and dwelling of an owner, his family, and his assistants began to be replaced by the 'lock-up' shop. Instead of being a life's work, shop-keeping was beginning to be an occupation with starting and finishing times, like any other.

The Times of 18 August 1902 referred to this trend:

> . . . the old-fashioned grocer who required to know many things about the 'art and mystery' of his trade [is being converted into] a vendor of packet goods so that a large proportion of the grocer's work of the present day could be accomplished almost equally well by an automatic machine delivering a packet of goods in exchange for a coin.

The 'Thunderer' was doubtless feeling cynical but could have had little idea how completely its forecast would be fulfilled half a century later!

Shops were being transformed gradually from establishments that existed solely to fulfil customers' known wants, into those designed and planned to attract customers and to create new wants. The crudest manifestation of this trend was in the employment of 'hookers-in' or pavement salesmen who did their utmost to get a customer inside the shop, leaving it to the salesman at the counter to finish off a 'kill'. But such methods were only used by small, less reputable shopkeepers.

A policy of clearly-marked fixed prices was becoming common in all trades, although the practice of auctioneering goods to clear stock at the end of the week was usual in the perishable food trades, particularly in butchery. The poor in cities did most of their shopping in the street; shops in certain areas catered only for the well-to-do and the growing middle classes.

In spite of the introduction of Bank Holidays, a weekly half-holiday, and controlled hours of work for young people, shop

assistants were still a depressed class. The *Daily Chronicle* published a number of articles at the turn of the century on conditions in shops. These show that bad living-in conditions, rushed meal-times, and irksome rules were still common features of life in shops where the employer or the shop-walker was tyrannical. Miss Margaret Bondfield, who had been a shop assistant and became Assistant Secretary of the National Union of Shop-Assistants and, later, the first woman Cabinet Minister in Britain, reported many examples of kindly employers and improving conditions of work, but these changes were very slow.

Before 1914 many shops were still social centres, where people went to pass the time of day, to gossip, and commiserate with one another over aches and pains or some family trouble, as much as to make a purchase. There was always plenty of time in those pre-refrigerator days, when shopping had to be done every day; and everything else must have had an enhanced value derived from this leisurely pace of life.

In the United States the trends were similar, but faster. In 1909 Henry Ford's first T model rolled off the assembly line and brought in rapid transportation for the masses, which helped to kill the country store. The car gave country people wider opportunities and they chose the chain store, the department store, and Woolworths. In his delightful book *The Old Country Store*, Gerald Carson wrote:

> Through all the years of its long life, there was little system or order in the country store. A great deal of time was wasted in looking for articles that were not in place, or had no place. Often the customer could find what he wanted more successfully than the merchant himself – an early version of self-service. Flies swarmed around the molasses barrel and there was never a mosquito bar to keep them off. There was tea in chests, packed in lead foil and straw matting with strange markings; rice and coffee

(*Opposite*)—London life at the turn of this century

57 The milkman
58 Covent Garden porters
59 Toyseller
60 Newsboys

61   A cockle stall before the First World War

62   London flower girls 1911

spilling out on the floor where a bag showed a rent; rum and brandy; harness and whale oil. The air was thick with an all-embracing odor, an aroma composed of dry herbs and wet dogs, of strong tobacco, green hides, and raw humanity. This redolence was to become famous in the annals of the country store as the assortment of goods grew wider and the smells more complex . . . Other methods of distributing goods came along to serve better the needs of the motor age. None ever equalled the original Pa and Ma store as a social as well as a commercial institution . . .

Open markets too were losing their importance as shopping centres and covered market halls were built in many towns in Britain at the turn of the century. These had the advantage of giving protection against the weather and of being open for trading throughout the week instead of on set days only.

The covered market halls were immensely popular with the working classes before 1914. They were places of entertainment as well as of buying and selling and on Saturday nights, in particular, they were crowded with men and women and their

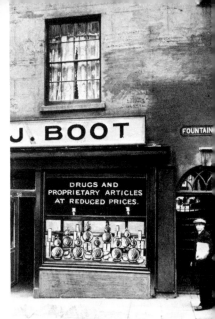

63   Jesse Boot's first chemist's shop in Nottingham

families who were looking for amusement as much as for
necessary goods to buy. Meat pies could be bought for 1d, there
were mussels and eels for sale, there were strong men performing
and fire swallowers and fortune tellers. In the Market Halls
Marks and Spencer's Penny Bazaars were one of the main
attractions and other tradesmen competed to be near them
because of the customers they always gathered.

Multiple shops in Britain can be traced back to the 1850s,
when the newsagent firms of W. H. Smith and Son and John
Menzies first began to build up their chains of bookstalls and
retail shops. These were a direct result of railway development
and reflected the growing numbers of people who travelled by
train and had time to spare on the journey for reading.

The grocery and footwear trades soon developed along the
same lines. By the end of the nineteenth century there were a
number of firms – the International Tea Company and
Freeman Hardy and Willis foremost among them – which had
over 100 branches each. By 1914 there were over 15 firms with
more than 200 branches and many with over 500 each.

64   One of the first Sainsbury shops in 1910

These multiple shop branches were spread fairly evenly among all the consumer goods trades and all over the country. They succeeded by purchasing in bulk on a scale formerly undreamed of, by rapid distribution of goods to a wide network of branches, by the development of close links with manufacturers and by a system of standardized stock control. Branches were situated mainly in working-class districts, where demand was limited to essentials and the emphasis was on cheapness and reliability.

The Co-operative movement did not attract mainly by charging low prices; its emphasis was on the 'dividend', on 'honest trading', and on the political doctrine of consumer control. The growth of 'Co-ops' tended therefore to be confined to the strongly homogeneous and more politically conscious working-class areas in the north of England and in Scotland, and its progress was slow in the shifting communities of the

Midlands and London. Multiple shops, on the other hand, did not depend upon loyalty and foresight among their customers and were able to expand in both south and north.

The importance of the specialist shop began to decline: many retailers began to 'poach' on the traditional selling lines of others and, gradually an entirely new type of retailer appeared – the chain store, which was essentially based on selling the products of a wide variety of different trades. This form of trading had started in the 1890s with the Penny Bazaars which Michael Marks first established in Manchester, and with the first British branch of Woolworths in Liverpool in 1909. Before 1914 put a check on further development, chain stores spread very quickly: men's outfitting, chemists' goods, tobacco, and stationery were the main lines involved.

Marks and Spencer's established an important position among chain stores, but they retained for a number of years features which had been characteristic of the market place and the market hall: open display, easy accessibility of goods, and self-selection. The typical Marks and Spencer bazaar before and during the First World War had a gangway running its entire length, with a horseshoe counter running round the three internal walls. On both sides of the entrance were counters opening on to the street, which were accessible to passers-by and could be closed at night by roll-top shutters. For a long time the bazaars displayed a sign 'Admission Free'.

The 'Great' War, as it was called until the Second came fast on its heels twenty years later, shattered the dream of automatic material progress which had been accepted without question in Edwardian Britain. The declaration of war on Germany was hailed with unthinking enthusiasm by many people, but the social implications of a modern conflict took everybody by surprise. As the French had done under Napoleon a century earlier, the Germans blockaded British ports and, by the use of the new submarine, cut food supplies so seriously that people went hungry, prices soared, and queues formed everywhere. Bread, in particular, rose in price and in January 1917 white bread was banned, and a 'standard' loaf, which included a proportion of barley, rice, oatmeal, beans, maize, and potato, was made compulsory. In November 1916 it was estimated that food prices had risen by 78 per cent since the beginning of the war, in November 1918, by 133 per cent.

65 A grocer's delivery boy in the 1930s. Delivering goods
is a much less common practice today

The years between the wars were a time of rapid change, in
spite of the tragedy of unemployment. The motor car, the radio,
the cinema, improvements in communications, the growth of
the popular press and of advertising all began to change
people's attitudes and ways of living and their shopping habits.
There was a great increase in the range, quality, and standard
of goods sold. Both imported and home-grown foods were
increasingly marked, graded, and identified by brand names.
There was a decrease in goods made or cooked in the home: the
kitchens and larders of the newer houses were stocked with
tins, containers, and packets weighing ounces and pounds,
instead of with sacks, bags, and drums weighing stones and
hundredweights.

But there was enormous suffering for many families in the
poorer areas. The daughter of an unemployed cotton worker in
Lancashire in the 1920s described the difficulties her mother
had in bringing up her family of three children:

> I think dole money was about 27s. 6d. for the family. I do not
> know how much [my father] got for Lloyd George [sickness
> benefit]. Rent was 7s. 6d. a week . . . Food was largely bread and
> potatoes . . . Once a week mother queued at the butcher and came

66   An early mobile shop to serve outlying districts

home if lucky with two-pennyworth of bacon bones, and made pea-soup for midday for all six. Eaten with or without bread. Hotpot and potato pie were favourite dishes . . . The chief difference between then and now [1968] is that one looked at every penny before spending it, and decided what was really essential. Milk was delivered in a churn in a horse-trap, and ladled out of the churn into a jug with a measure. The housewife had to go out to the cart every morning and buy as much as she needed, rather than leave a standing order . . . Newspaper was a favourite wrapping, and nothing was sealed. Sugar and flour were sold loose from the sacks. Butter was cut off a huge piece (56 lbs) and slapped with butter pats . . . Shopping was slow as everything had to be weighed.[1]

The growing use of the motor car had an important effect on the location of shops and the types of service which shopkeepers could provide for their customers. Middle-class customers began to be increasingly attracted away from local shops and drove longer distances to brighter, better laid-out ones in main street sites. Department Stores began to open branches in medium-sized provincial towns and in suburban districts of large towns. Their major attraction continued to be the wide range of goods they stocked, their effective display, and the

[1] Quoted in *English Homes and Housekeeping* by Barbara Megson, Routledge and Kegan Paul 1968.

67   Christmas shopping in Kensington High Street,
London, from *The Sphere*, 1925

freedom of customers to inspect without any obligation to buy.
Amenities such as rest-rooms, public telephones, and restaurants
made large store shopping pleasant and enjoyable.

There were great advances too, in the standard of shop-
window display in the 1930s. The window dresser was now a
trained employee and attractive windows, lit by electricity,
combined with cleanliness, good layout, and fittings became
important factors in attracting customers.

The Second World War proved to be a watershed in shopping and consumer affairs, as in much else. Remembering the
food shortages of the First World War and the near-starvation
which the German blockade had brought to Britain, the
government brought in food rationing long before food became
short. From January 1940 ration cards had to be produced for
basic foodstuffs. In 1941 the weekly allowances for each adult
were 4 ounces of bacon or ham, 8 ounces of sugar, 2 ounces of
tea, 8 ounces of fats, of which only 2 ounces could be of butter,
2 ounces of jam, 1 ounce of cheese and a shilling's worth of
meat. Later, sweets and tinned goods were obtainable only on
a 'points' system; bread was not rationed until after the war – in
July 1946.

On 1 June 1941 the newspapers carried the following detailed
announcement from the Board of Trade:

RATIONING

of Clothing, Cloth, Footwear
from June 1, 1941

Rationing has been introduced, not to deprive you of your real needs, but to make more certain that you get your share of the country's goods – to get fair shares with everybody else.

When the shops re-open you will be able to buy cloth, clothes, footwear and knitting wool only if you bring your Food Ration Book with you. The shopkeeper will detach the required number of coupons from the unused margarine page. Each margarine coupon counts as one coupon towards the purchase of clothing or footwear. You will have a total of 66 coupons to last you for a year; so go sparingly. You can buy where you like and when you like without registering.

NUMBER OF COUPONS NEEDED

Men and Boys	Adult	Child	Women and Girls	Adult	Child
Unlined mackintosh or cape	9	7	Lined mackintoshes or coats (over 28 in. in length)	14	11
Other mackintoshes, or raincoat, or overcoat	16	11	Jacket or short coat (under 28 in. in length)	11	8
Coat, or jacket, or blazer or like garment	13	8	Dress, or gown, or frock – woollen	11	8
Waistcoat, or pull-over, or cardigan or jersey	5	3	Dress, or gown, or frock – other material	7	5
Trousers (other than fustian or corduroy)	8	6	Gym tunic, or girl's skirt with bodice	8	6
Fustian or corduroy trousers	5	5	Blouse, or sports shirt, or cardigan or jumper	5	3
Shorts	5	3	Skirt or divided skirt	7	5
Overalls, or dungarees, or like garment	6	4	Overalls or dungarees, or like garment	6	4
Dressing gown or bathing gown	8	6	Apron or pinafore	3	2
Night-shirt or pair of pyjamas	8	6	Pyjamas	8	6
Shirt, or combinations – woollen	8	6	Nightdress	6	5
Shirt, or combinations – other material	5	4	Petticoat, or slip, or combination, or cami-knickers	4	3
			Other garments, including corsets	5	2
			Pair of stockings	2	1
			Pair of socks (ankle		

Pants, or vest, or bathing costume, or child's blouse	4	2
Pair of socks or stockings	3	1
Collar, or tie, or pair of cuffs	1	1
Two handkerchiefs	1	1
Scarf, or pair of gloves or mittens	2	2
Pair of slippers or galoshes	4	2
Pair of boots or shoes	7	3
Pair of leggings, gaiters, or spats	3	2
length)	1	1
Two handkerchiefs	1	1
Scarf, or pair of gloves or mittens or muff	2	2
Pair of slippers, boots or shoes	5	3

CLOTH. Coupons needed per yard depend on the width. For example, a yard of woollen cloth 36 inches wide requires 3 coupons. The same amount of cotton or other cloth needs 2 coupons.

KNITTING WOOL 1 coupon for two ounces.

THESE GOODS MAY BE BOUGHT WITHOUT COUPONS
Children's clothing of sizes generally suitable for infants less than 4 years old. Boiler suits and workmen's bib and brace overalls. Hats and caps. Sewing thread. Mending wool and mending silk. Boot and shoe laces. Tapes, braids, ribbons and other fabrics of 3 inches or less in width. Elastic. Lace and lace net. Sanitary towels. Braces, suspenders and garters. Hard haberdashery. Clogs. Black-out cloth dyed black. All second-hand articles.

SPECIAL NOTICE TO RETAILERS

Retailers will be allowed to get fresh stocks of cloth up to and including June 28th, of other rationed goods up to and including June 21st., WITHOUT SURRENDERING COUPONS. After those dates they will be able to obtain fresh stocks only by turning in their customers' coupons. Steps have been taken, in the interest of the smaller retailers, to limit during these periods the quantity of goods which can be supplied by a wholesaler or manufacturer to any one retailer, however large his orders. Further information can be obtained from your Trade Organisations.

Life during the war was drab, but far from dull. The bombing brought excitement as well as much distress and there was a certain heightening of awareness in the recurring dangers; one

68 A friendly corner shop of the early 1950s. Compare
with No. 73

69 Notice the crowded display of goods in this small
draper's shop of the same period

realized each morning that one was indeed lucky to be alive.
But food and clothing were monotonous and much 'making do'
had to be resorted to if there was to be enough. Many reconsti-
tuted and 'mock' foods were produced: dehydrated milk and
eggs, dried potato, whale meat, spam, and a curious fish called
'snoek'. Clothes rationing encouraged inventiveness and many
were the dresses made from curtains, and curtains made from
floorcloths or similar unrationed material. There was fun in
having to 'make do' – as there always is.

The cost of the war was astronomical and had to be paid for
from dwindling foreign investments and from new loans from
the United States and Canada. But these had to be repaid and
for some years after the war there were few, if any, luxuries
about and even necessities were in short supply. Shopping was
a very restricted activity for some years.

The prolonged shortage of food in Britain was due in part to
the needs of the rest of war-torn Europe. Farming in Britain had
been revitalized by wartime needs, but in Europe it had
suffered badly and millions of people were in danger of starva-
tion. Emergency supplies of food and medical goods had to be
provided for desperate people, friends and enemies alike.

Imports of food were severely restricted; in 1947 Government
posters announced: 'Britain must earn her keep . . . we cannot
buy anything we cannot afford to pay for'.

70 Woolworth's '3d and 6d stores' now sell almost anything. Notice the organized layout for a quick turnover of stock

Clothes came off ration in March 1949 and sweets in May 1953. By 1951 a few luxuries were coming back into the shops and a new era of affluence was dawning. The Festival of Britain showed that the spirit of enterprise and achievement was still as vigorous as it had been a century earlier at the time of the Great Exhibition. Many new discoveries were on show, polythene and other plastics foremost among them, all of which have transformed the shopping scene ever since.

A few years later, Sir Alec Clegg, Director of Education for the West Riding of Yorkshire, reminded an audience of some of the vast changes which thirty years had brought in employment, and therefore in the goods on which people spend their money:

Since those days . . . we in western civilization have undergone an amazing revolution . . . The census figures tell the dramatic story . . . [in 1931] there were in this country 128,000 drivers of horse-drawn vehicles and in 1961 there were not enough of them to make a separate category, but there were 41,000 radio and radar mechanics who hardly existed 30 years ago. There were

71 An antiques stall in the Portobello street market, London

57,000 fewer blacksmiths, 27,000 fewer coachbuilders, 286,000 fewer hewers of coal. But there were 447,000 more draughtsmen, 75,000 more mechanical and electrical engineers, 24,000 more doctors, and our increased affluence showed itself in 56,000 more hairdressers, beauticians, manicurists and chiropodists.[1]

The 1960s saw a revolution in shopping habits – a revolution which is far from spent. A fundamental break with the past is taking place before our eyes. Shops are getting fewer; whereas in 1960 there were 542,000 shops in Britain, by 1975 the number is expected to drop to 450,000. Shops are getting bigger, and most of them sell a much wider variety of goods than they used to do. Many shops are moving from city and town centres into suburban or even rural situations where rents are lower and they can offer customers plenty of parking space.

In all countries, Government and Local Authorities are faced with a great many decisions which will affect the pattern of shopping in the future. Whereas in the past it was the consumer who decided the pace and shape of change, increasingly it is the planners and the property developers who dictate where and

[1] Quoted Megson, *Op. Cit.* p 80.

how shops shall be built, and on what scale. This is one of the prices that we, in western industrial societies, have to pay for a steadily increasing standard of living.

One important sociological factor which influences the development of shops is the increase in the number of wives who work. Homes with two wage-earners have a higher level of disposable income; working wives have more money to spend and less time in which to spend it; they want to do their shopping as quickly and efficiently as possible and all in one trip. They want, too, to shop after work and more and more of them want to be able to park a car very near the shops.

The future was mapped out when self-service shops first appeared in the United States and were accepted by the majority of housewives. The next stage was to expand the shopping space until it covered a shopping area of over 2,000 square feet, still run on the self-service principle, and so supermarkets sprang up in every High Street, cutting costs by operating on a larger scale, buying in bulk, and dispensing with individual service.

The success of supermarkets was based on a more efficient use of labour. As a result the shopper gets more hygienic conditions, little or no waiting, a choice from an astonishing range of pre-packed foods, the possibility of doing all her shopping under one roof, and leisure to choose more than she intends. These advantages tend to be forgotten in the controversy over prices, but they are important parts of one-stop shopping appeal. Fewer and fewer shops are friendly social units; more and more resemble factories, with their space costed, productivity measured and stocks controlled. Shopping is fast becoming an assembly line operation, instead of the social ritual it was for centuries.

But the success of supermarkets has been in many cases less than expected. The spread of car ownership tends to choke town centres with traffic and has made it essential to ban parking in main streets. Customers are often reduced to parking well away from their supermarket, leaving bulging shopping bags on the pavement while they collect their car and hope they will be able to pull up alongside.

A very popular new way of shopping is in a Shopping Centre, made up of a variety of shops, either under a single roof or round a precinct. One of the newest of these, Shopping City,

72 Pedestrian precinct in an old shopping area of Harlow New Town. Such precincts are becoming more popular as traffic congestion increases in towns

73 Shopping today: efficient? Quick? Easy? Cheaper? Unfriendly?

at Runcorn in Lancashire, is the biggest covered shopping centre in Europe, faced with gleaming white self-cleaning ceramic tiles which are guaranteed to stay white. It is a real town centre, with cafes and a pub, two studio cinemas, the headquarters of the social services, a bingo hall, restaurant, dance hall, and squash courts. There are cleverly sited car parks, with total space for over 2,000 cars, set at each corner of the site so that parking is easy from whichever way the car-borne shopper approaches. A fast busway runs in a figure of eight round both old and new Runcorn and into the Shopping City, and from it passengers step into a covered terminal and go by covered escalators to the 100 or so shops. There is underground access to all the shops so that no delivery traffic is ever seen by shoppers in the City.

During the nineteen-fifties out-of-town stores took the United States and Canada by storm. It was realized that land is cheaper outside towns, access is easier, plentiful parking can be provided, and customers are attracted by lower prices, longer opening hours, and the convenience of one-stop shopping. The buildings tend to be huge, stark, without decorations or advertisements, so costs are cut to the bone.

These 'hypermarkets' were not known in Europe until the 1960s; now they are highly successful in Germany, France, Belgium, Sweden, Austria, Holland, Norway, and Denmark.

A strong argument against hypermarkets is that they are bound to syphon off trade from town centres and local shops, and thus worsen a trend which is already making shopping more difficult for those who have no car. Others fear that a growth of out of town shopping areas may contribute to the decay of city centres as has undoubtedly happened in the United States. On environmental grounds there is only room for a limited number of hypermarkets in a small country like England. A British Minister for the Environment, voiced a general disquiet when he stated recently:

> Over-provision of shops on a large scale and the loss of trade by town and district centres which are at present well served by public transport could change the character of these centres and have serious consequences to which local planning authorities must have regard.

The battle is joined, with the customer neatly placed in between the two main protagonists. We have to face up to the question of just how much we are prepared to pay, in environmental terms, for our general affluence.

There are other, very competitive methods of retailing which are fighting to get hold of the consumer's money. Discount trading has become widespread in large cities and has undoubted attractions. This is not a new phenomenon, but modern discounting really got under way in England in 1964, when the abolition of retail price maintenance allowed retailers to charge competitive prices.

Most discounters operate from a form of shop-warehouse away from a town centre but near a main road. They can sell to the public far more cheaply than a department store because they tend to specialize, to buy in enough bulk to be able to negotiate on manufacturers' prices, and have much lower overheads. Prices are of course lower as larger quantities are bought, a large amount of time is saved, and there are growing numbers of women who share their purchases and the cost of petrol and shop once a month.

So the wheel has come full circle: in earlier times when most food was grown or made at home shopping was an occasional event; mass production, urban living, and the spread of shops led to the habit of frequent, small shopping expeditions and the resulting interest and social enrichment; now the motor car and the deep freeze enable the housewife to revert to the habits of pre-industrial days and again – but for entirely different reasons – to shop only occasionally.

Competing against all kinds of shops and taking a growing share of retail trade are the mail order businesses, a high proportion of which are in clothing and footwear. According to the Mail Order Traders' Association, some 16 per cent of all women's clothing and 25 per cent of household textiles are purchased through mail order catalogues. A growing volume of mail order business is conducted by specialized organizations which advertise single items in newspapers and magazines and ask for cash with orders.

Direct selling will always have a place in the distributive system, but during recent years a new type of skilled rogue has been operating. Pyramid sellers make money by persuading people to pay large sums for the right to act as distributors for products which can have very little market potential. They are also paid for recruiting new agents. A tragic characteristic of pyramid selling is that victims not only lose money in buying themselves into the scheme, but they may also, because of the recruitment incentive, risk losing their friends. Authorities are rightly concerned about the hardships which pyramid selling has caused and are committed to taking measures to outlaw the practice, though this is difficult.

The changes in Britain's shopping habits over the past decade have not all been caused by spreading branches of chain stores or by supermarkets. Quietly and gradually the pattern of small shop ownership has been changing too. The growing influx of Greek, Italian, West Indian, Pakistani, and Indian traders, catering principally for their own countrymen, gives a slightly exotic air to many suburban shopping streets, and many Chinese take-away food shops serve customers at all hours.

This ethnic business world has achieved its profitability by dint of one thing above all – the capacity of these traders and shop-keepers to work hard for long hours and to make profits where so many traditional small shop-owners have failed. Families and relatives are not so demanding on the wages front and they generally work harder for their own kith and kin than outsiders would do.

Supermarketing, the journal of the large-scale food retailing world, has recently predicted that the milkman's daily delivery will soon disappear in England. Now that Britain has joined the European Economic Community, continental patterns of milk consumption are bound to have an important influence. Almost all other countries use the bulk of their milk to make cheese, butter, milk powder, and other milk-based products such as flavoured milk drinks and yogurt. In most of Europe only 30 to 35 per cent of milk is actually drunk; in Britain the figure is 70 per cent. Only some 8 per cent of this is sold through shops, the rest is brought to the door by milkmen. Milk rounds in business districts are already uneconomic and some people in the dairy industry predict that city milk rounds will soon disappear; people living in cities will become accustomed to buying their milk from supermarkets, so 'no-delivery' areas are bound to grow. People will be fortunate too, in a few years time, if papers and letters are delivered to their door.

Our very advantages can be problems. Even in our affluent society – perhaps indeed partly because of our affluence – there are many consumer frustrations nowadays. Automatic vending

74   Street traders in Oxford Street, London

machines often break down or are damaged; gift coupons and
trading 'stamps' of all kinds are a confusion – a nonsense to
some people but an excitement to many; the wide choice that
faces every shopper can often inhibit sensible decisions; and the
ease and extent of hire purchase shopping are a trap for too
many. The average consumer does not know how to make
effective complaints about unsatisfactory purchases and tends
too often to judge everything on price.

In England, the Consumer Association and their magazine
Which? have for many years given invaluable advice to sub-
scribers; the Council of Industrial Design, their Design Centres,
and their many publications are all working towards the crea-
tion of a better-informed and therefore more discriminating
shopping public. Many unnecessary complexities of consumer
law have been swept away by the 1973 Fair Trading Act, which
has been described as the most comprehensive measure of

consumer protection ever introduced. The Director-General of Fair Trading will watch out for all consumer trade practices which may react unfairly upon shoppers and in future no amount of legal phraseology will enable a seller to avoid his responsibility to supply goods of 'merchantable' quality. Whether the consumer pays cash or buys under credit sale or by hire purchase, he or she will in future have the same basic right to expect a fair deal from the supplier.

It is astonishing to realize that over half the goods being sold in modern shops are post-war discoveries. How did people manage to live without detergents, frozen foods, plastic kitchenware, paper handkerchiefs, non-iron shirts, creaseless skirts, fake furs, laminated surfaces, spin driers, nylon tights, ball-point pens, instant coffee, transistor radio sets, electric shavers, and much else?

Modern industrial society is geared to mass production and this inevitably means a rapid turnover and consequent obsolescence. Our ancestors would not have understood at all the idea of obsolescence: they repaired, tinkered, turned, patched, and generally made do. We think it a freedom not to have to do so.

The late Raymond Chandler in *The Long Good-bye* had this to say:

> [A newspaper tycoon is talking to the detective, Philip Marlowe] You can't have quality with mass production. You don't want it because it lasts too long. So you substitute styling, which is a commercial swindle intended to produce artificial obsolescence. Mass production couldn't sell its goods next year unless it made what is sold this year look unfashionable a year from now. We have the whitest kitchens and the most shining bathrooms in the world. But in the lovely white kitchen the average American housewife can't produce a meal fit to eat, and the lovely shining bathroom is mostly a receptacle for deodorants, laxatives, sleeping pills, and the products of that confidence racket called the cosmetic industry. We make the finest packages in the world, Mr. Marlowe. The stuff inside is mostly junk.[1]

Fortunately not yet true – but the danger is clear.

[1] *The Long Goodbye* by Raymond Chandler, Hamish Hamilton, 1953.

A List of Books

EARLY BOOKS

Geoffrey Chaucer. *The Canterbury Tales*
Froissart. *Chronicles*
Harrison. *Description of England*, 1577–1587
Holinshed. *Chronicles*, 1577
Stubbes. *Anatomy of the Abuses in England*, 1583
Stow. *A Survey of London*, 1598
Platter. *Travels in England*, 1599
Dekker. *The Gull's Horn Book*, 1609
Dunton. *Life and Errors of John Dunton*, 1705
N.H. *The Compleat Tradesman*, 1684
Defoe. *The Compleat English Tradesman*, 1727
de la Roche. *Sophie in London*, 1786
Waller. *A General Description of all Trades*, 1747
North. *Lives of the Norths*, 1826
Mayhew. *London Labour and London Poor*, 1861
Rye. *England as Seen by Foreigners*, 1865
Rogers. *A History of Agriculture and Prices*, 1866
Riley. *Memorials of London and London Life*, 1868
Barnard. *Medieval England* (?), 1860
Traill. *Social England*, 1897

RECENT BOOKS

Salzman. *English Trade in the Middle Ages*, 1931
Power. *Medieval People*, 1924
Bennett. *The Pastons and their England*, 1922
Kingsford. *Prejudice and Promise in 15th Century England*, 1925
Lambert. *The Universal Provider*, 1938
Drummond and Wilbraham. *The Englishmans Food*, 1939
Levy. *The Shops of Britain*, 1948
Davis. *A History of Shopping*, 1966
Mitchell and Leys. *A History of London Life*, 1958
Owen. *The Life of Robert Owen, by Himself*, ed. 1920
The Household Book of Sarah Fell, ed. 1921
The Northumberland Household Book, ed. 1905
Power and Postan. *English Trade in the Fifteenth Century*, 1933
Klingender. *The Little Shop*, 1951
Scott Thompson. *Life in a Noble Household*, 1937
The Stonor Letters and Papers, ed. 1919
Whitaker. *Victorian and Edwardian Shop Workers*, 1973
Heal. *London Tradesmen's Cards of the 18th century*, 1925
Rees. *St Michael: A History of Marks & Spencers*, 1969
Millar. *The Affluent Sheep*, 1963
Willian. *An eighteenth century Shop-keeper. Abraham Dent of Kirby Stephen*, 1970
Packard. *The Hidden Persuaders*, 1956
Packard. *The Waste Makers*, 1970

Acknowledgements

THE AUTHOR AND PUBLISHERS wish to record their grateful thanks to copyright owners for the use of the illustrations listed below:

B. T. Batsford Ltd. for: 38
Bibliothèque, Paris for: 11
Boots Ltd. for: 63
British Museum for: 6, 7
Camera Press for: 71, 74, 75
Greater London Council for: 41, 49
The London Museum for: 1, 20, 21, 27, 30, 32, 33, 36, 40, 42, 46, 47, 54, 55, 61, 67
Mansell Collection for: 10, 12, 19, 22, 23, 35, 48, 52, 65, 66, 69
Marks and Spencer Ltd. for: 13
Mary Evans Picture Library for: 43
John McCann for: 72
Museum of the City of New York for: 31, 51, 53, 76
The National Gallery for: 28
Collection of the Newark Museum, U.S.A. for: 2
New York Historical Society, New York City for: title page
Palazzo Ducale Venezia for: 17
Radio Times Hulton Picture Library for: 4, 9, 13, 14, 15, 16, 24, 26, 34, 37, 39, 44, 50, 62, 68
J. Sainsbury Ltd. for: 64
Stimson Photo Collection, Wyoming State Archives and Historical Department for: 45
Trinity College Cambridge for: 5
Victoria and Albert Museum for: 18, 29, 56
F. W. Woolworth & Co. Ltd. for: 70

75 Boutique shopping

Index

Page numbers given in italics refer to illustrations

76   A country store in The Bronx
at the turn of the century

Printed in Great Britain
by The Bowering Press Limited, Plymouth